CAMBRIDGE LIBRARY COLLECTION

Books of enduring scholarly value

Slavery and Abolition

The books reissued in this series include accounts of historical events and movements by eye-witnesses and contemporaries, as well as landmark studies that assembled significant source materials or developed new historiographical methods. The series includes work in social, political and military history on a wide range of periods and regions, giving modern scholars ready access to influential publications of the past.

Facts and Documents Connected with the Late Insurrection in Jamaica

The Christmas Rebellion (1831–2) saw the uprising of 60,000 Jamaican slaves, many of them followers of one Baptist preacher. Initially intended only as a peaceful strike, it escalated as estates were burned down and plantation owners killed. This 1832 pamphlet details the violence and persecution directed against nonconformists and missionaries, who were regarded as having been sympathetic towards the revolt. The materials were published by William Knibb, a Baptist minister, who in 1832 was summoned to appear before parliamentary committees investigating the state of the Caribbean colonies. His evidence and the rebellion itself are regarded as having quickened the pace of emancipation in Jamaica. The documents are reissued here with an 1837 narrative by James Williams, a youth who became an apprentice under the system that replaced slavery. He describes how conditions for former slaves were little improved, with many instances of harsh treatment and unjust imprisonment.

T0364274

Cambridge University Press has long been a pioneer in the reissuing of out-of-print titles from its own backlist, producing digital reprints of books that are still sought after by scholars and students but could not be reprinted economically using traditional technology. The Cambridge Library Collection extends this activity to a wider range of books which are still of importance to researchers and professionals, either for the source material they contain, or as landmarks in the history of their academic discipline.

Drawing from the world-renowned collections in the Cambridge University Library and other partner libraries, and guided by the advice of experts in each subject area, Cambridge University Press is using state-of-the-art scanning machines in its own Printing House to capture the content of each book selected for inclusion. The files are processed to give a consistently clear, crisp image, and the books finished to the high quality standard for which the Press is recognised around the world. The latest print-on-demand technology ensures that the books will remain available indefinitely, and that orders for single or multiple copies can quickly be supplied.

The Cambridge Library Collection brings back to life books of enduring scholarly value (including out-of-copyright works originally issued by other publishers) across a wide range of disciplines in the humanities and social sciences and in science and technology.

Facts and Documents Connected with the Late
Insurrection in Jamaica

*With a Narrative of Events
since the First of August, 1834*

Anon.
James Williams

CAMBRIDGE
UNIVERSITY PRESS

CAMBRIDGE UNIVERSITY PRESS

Cambridge, New York, Melbourne, Madrid, Cape Town,
Singapore, São Paolo, Delhi, Mexico City

Published in the United States of America by Cambridge University Press, New York

www.cambridge.org
Information on this title: www.cambridge.org/9781108053143

© in this compilation Cambridge University Press 2012

This edition first published 1837
This digitally printed version 2012

ISBN 978-1-108-05314-3 Paperback

FACTS AND DOCUMENTS

CONNECTED WITH THE

LATE INSURRECTION IN JAMAICA,

AND THE

VIOLATIONS OF CIVIL AND RELIGIOUS LIBERTY

ARISING OUT OF IT.

ADVERTISEMENT.

THE following Publication owes its appearance to the suggestions of many esteemed friends, who are desirous that the British Public at large should be more fully acquainted with the nature and origin of the recent disturbances in Jamaica, especially in their aspect on the religious instruction of the negroes. The various documents are printed, as much as possible, in their original form, and without the least attempt to weave them into a continuous narrative. It would have been easy greatly to increase their number, especially under Sections II. and III.; but these, it is presumed, will be sufficient to demonstrate how formidable are the obstacles which impede the progress of the Gospel in Jamaica, and to combine all the friends of humanity, freedom, and religion, in a vigorous effort to remove them.

SECTION I.

Memorial and Statement of the Baptist Missionaries in Jamaica, dated 19th April, 1832;

TO

HIS EXCELLENCY EARL BELMORE,

The Governor of Jamaica.

The Humble Memorial of the undersigned Baptist Missionaries, Sheweth,

THAT on the 13th February last, a Memorial, signed by certain of your present Memorialists, was presented to your Excellency, stating, among other things, that their Property had been plundered, " several of their Chapels totally demolished, their persons threatened with violence, under the countenance and with the aid of Magistrates and Officers of Militia," and praying, in the apprehension of the continuance of similar acts of wanton outrage against their property and lives, for the interposition of your Excellency's authority and power to protect them.

A

That, in answer to that Memorial, your then Memorialists received a Letter from your Excellency's Secretary, apprizing them that its prayer had been anticipated in the issuing and promulgation throughout the Island, of a Proclamation on the subject, of which a Copy was enclosed.

That your Memorialists felt grateful to your Excellency for the strong terms of condemnation in which that Proclamation spoke of the wanton and illegal "destruction of their Chapels and Places of Worship,—proceedings, as your Excellency not more strongly than justly characterized them, disgraceful to the Colony, subversive of order, and of dangerous example." And your Memorialists did fain hope that the protection which they were seeking at your Excellency's hands, would be actually afforded them in the obedience which would be paid by the "Custodes of Parishes and all Magistrates" to the injunctions laid upon them in that Proclamation "to seek out and discover the authors of these outrages, that they might be punished according to law;" and "to employ the whole force which the Constitution has entrusted to them in protecting Property of every description, whether belonging to private persons or religious societies; in quelling all disorderly meetings, and in bringing to exemplary punishment every disturber of the public peace." But whatever confidence your Memorialists may have had in a ready attention, on the part of those persons, to your Excellency's orders, and to the due execution of their duties as the legally constituted and sworn preservers of the public peace : the result has proved it to have been in most cases totally unfounded.

That, from many of the circumstances detailed in the accompanying Statement of various outrages and indignities to which they have been subjected—of reiterated attacks upon their lives and property (which your Memorialists conceive must be known to your Excellency, since they are of public notoriety,) it is evident that the Civil and Local Military Authorities in many parishes of the Island, with but few exceptions, have treated and do still treat your Excellency's Proclamation and Authority with contempt. It is equally evident that, so far from the first of these affording your Memorialists the protection they required, and as British Subjects are entitled to, the impunity with which it has been disregarded, indeed trampled on, by the very persons to whom it was addressed, is a strong encouragement to them and others to proceed to further acts of wanton aggression and threatened violence. Your Memorialists therefore are again obliged to approach your Excellency with the expression of their fears, (which surely cannot now be deemed ill-founded) that, unless a more effectual exertion of your Authority is interposed, as heretofore, so in future their property and persons will lie entirely, as far at least as the laws which should protect them are concerned, at the mercy of a deeply prejudiced, an unprincipled and lawless party which is intent upon their destruction. And your Memorialists submit to your Excellency that it is a case calling for your serious attention, and for the exercise of your High Powers, when, in a British Colony, and under a British Governor and British Laws, British Subjects against whom not a single charge can be substantiated, dare not return to their homes and their functions, but with the certain expectation of suffering personal violence under the wilful connivance, if not immediate sanction of the very persons to whom as Magistrates the preservation of the public peace is committed. Though they trust there are some honorable exceptions, your Memorialists speak advisedly in bringing this charge against the Magistracy generally, of the parishes in which the outrages detailed in the accompanying Statement have occurred, and for their full justification in bringing it they humbly beg to refer your Excellency to the particulars of those outrages, and to the fact that not a single attempt of any one Custos or Magistrate to seek out and discover their authors, that they might be punished according to law, in compliance with the proclamation, has yet come to their knowledge.

That your Memorialists now approach your Excellency, humbly but earnestly to seek that effectual protection to which, in common with their fellow subjects, they feel themselves entitled, and which under the circumstances, none but your Excellency can afford. They detail specific grounds of complaint. They look to your Excellency for the redress of their grievances, by the exercise of the power with which their gracious Sovereign has invested you for the protection of all his faithful subjects in this Colony, and for the punishment of every con-temner of the laws. They desire to do so respectfully; but they must at the same time solemnly tell your Excellency, that having now adopted every means in their power to place themselves under the protection of the laws by which they are governed, they are about to resume their duties at some of the stations which injustice and cruelty compelled them to leave, in the exercise of an indefeasible right belonging to every Briton, and in the consciousness that whatever consequences may ensue to themselves or others in the execution of any of the threats of violence so publicly held out, the blame and the guilt cannot lie upon them.

That your Memorialists in furnishing the accompanying Statement are actuated by the hope that your Excellency will see the necessity for now adopting such measures as will effectually redress the past injuries inflicted on the religious body of which they are members, in the destruction of their chapels and other property, and as will ensure them against future acts of oppression and outrage.

Your Memorialists therefore humbly pray your Excellency to extend to them such relief as to your Excellency shall seem meet.

And your Memorialists shall ever pray, &c.

JOSHUA TINSON,	FRANCIS GARDNER,
WILLIAM KNIBB,	WM. WHITEHORNE,
EDWARD BAYLIS,	THOS. F. ABBOTT,
JOSEPH BURTON,	JOSIAH BARLOW,
HENRY C. TAYLOR,	WALTER DENDY,
SAMUEL NICHOLLS,	JOHN KINGDON.
JOHN CLARKE,	

Statement referred to in the Memorial.

DURING Martial Law, the following Property, in which the Baptist Missionaries were interested, was destroyed by the Militia.

A New Chapel called *Salter's Hill*, in St. James's, just completed, was set fire to by a party of the St. James's Militia, under the command of F. B. Gibbs, Esq. and Captain George Gordon.

A Private House in St. James's, called *Putney*, rented as a place of worship; and a residence called *Hillington*, in Hanover; the property of

Mr. Burchell, were severally burnt by the Militia; and a house in Hanover, called *Shepherd's Hall,* hired as a place of worship, was entered by the Militia, and the Pews, Furniture, and Pulpit therein, belonging to Mr. Burchell, were taken out and burnt.

On the 8th February last, the Baptist Chapel at Montego Bay, was pulled down at mid-day, by a large mob, among whom were the following Magistrates, and Officers of Militia, most of whom were very actively engaged.—

Lieut.-Col.	Wm. Charles Morris,	
Major	John Coates,	
Captain	George Gordon,	
,,	Wm. Mitchell Kerr,	*Magistrates.*
,,	John Cleghorn,	
,,	John Bowen,	
,,	Benjamin Haughton Tharpe,	
,,	Wm. Nettleton Balme.	
,,	John Tharpe,	*A Magistrate.*
,,	Edward Evans,	*Coroner.*
Lieut.	James Gordon,	*A Magistrate.*
,,	Joseph Fray.	
,,	William Plummer.	
,,	Thomas Watson.	
,,	Charles Wallace Ogle.	
,,	John Henry Morris.	
,,	George M'Farquhar Lawson, jun. (Adjutant.)	
Lieut.	Henry Hunter.	
Ensign	William Fowle Holt.	
,,	James Coates.	
,,	William Gordon.	
,,	Joseph Gill Jump.	

Alexander Campbell, Esq. (Copse)
Charles O'Conner, Esq.   *Magistrates.*
William Heath, Esq.
William B. Popkin, the Head Constable.

This outrage occurred within two hours after the Custos, and Dr. G. M. Lawson, Colonel of the St. James's Regiment, and a Magistrate also, had been informed that it was about to take place, yet the parties met with no interruption in their proceedings.

The perpetrators of this act are well known at Montego Bay, and no difficulties whatever exist in the way of " discovering the authors of the outrage."

The Proclamation of the 13th February was posted about the Town of Montego Bay, but within an hour after it was torn down.

On the 14th March, the lodgings of Mr. Burchell, a Baptist Missionary, (the indictment against whom had been that day ignored) was approached by a mob, composed chiefly of white persons, for the purpose, as they said, of doing him some bodily injury, and but for the voluntary opposition offered by private persons, all their purposes would have been effected before a Magistrate came to the spot, and during the time occupied by some of the authorities in procuring affidavits of Mr. Burchell's danger, which they required though they saw him surrounded by the mob, before they would call in a military guard. Mr. Burchell was obliged to quit the Island, for the preservation of his life.

On the night of the 12th February, the Baptist Chapel at Rio Bueno was attacked and partially destroyed by the Grenadier Company of the Trelawney Regiment, (dressed in their regimentals,) which was stationed at Bryan Castle Estate, near that place, and on the evening of the 18th it was burnt down.

On the —— February the Chapel at Stewart Town, in Trelawney, was partially pulled down by some persons also connected with the militia.

The Baptist Chapel at Falmouth had been occupied during Martial Law as Barracks by the St. Ann's Regiment. On the 7th February, when that Corps was about to quit the Town, Mr. John W. Gayner, a Magistrate, and Ensign; and Adjutant Samuel Tucker, commanded the men to break down the Chapel, and themselves set the example, saying, " these were the orders they had received."—It was completely demolished.

While the work of destruction was proceeding, information was given to Lieut. Thomas Tennison, of the Trelawney Regiment, the officer on guard in the Town. His reply was, that " it was no matter whether they broke it or not, he supposed they would set it on fire too !"

Mr. Knibb, one of the Missionaries, paid a visit to Falmouth, early in March. For three successive nights his lodging was stoned, and he was cautioned by two respectable gentlemen, against venturing out in the evening, as a party had clubbed together to tar and feather him.

After Martial Law was discontinued, the horses of Mr. Knibb were taken from Falmouth, by Major General Hilton, who has, until very recently, retained possession of them.

At Lucea, on the 6th January, Lieut.-Colonel John Edward Payne, and Major Richard Chambers (Magistrates,) and Mr. Heath, (the Rector) went to Mr. Abbott, (the Baptist Missionary's Residence) and stated that he had run away. Mr. Payne asked if he had any letters from Burchell, and said, " The Baptists had tried to ruin them, but instead of that the Baptists would be ruined themselves."

Mr. Chambers opened Mrs. Abbott's desk with a false key, though he was told it was hers, and searched her letters. They locked, nailed, and sealed up the doors, and windows of the house, and used a great deal of abusive language to Miss Dickson, who had charge of his house. Mr. Heath took away Mr. Abbott's church books, which have never been returned.

On Thursday, February 9th, in the morning, the Baptist Chapel at Lucea, was destroyed; the following parties were among the perpetrators of the outrage :—

Mr. B. Heath (the Rector.)
Doctor Binns,
Charles Younger, (Constable.)

Mr. Alexander Campbell, of Lucea, (a Magistrate) was present, and did not attempt to prevent it.

Mr. Heath, (Rector) asked a gentleman to go with him, and assist him in destroying " the d——d Baptist Chapel."

Mr. Richard Chambers, on the evening of the same day, refused to exercise his authority as a Magistrate, when Mr. Abbott's dwelling-house was violently entered by Dr. Binns and others, armed with hatchets, &c. for the purpose of destroying his furniture. On this occasion a respectable female, attempting to protect Mr. Abbott's property, was struck with a horsewhip, by Dr. Binns, who threatened to push her down the steps if she did not go.

Several dozens of wine were destroyed, and some of Mr. Abbott's books and clothes stolen.

On Friday night, February 10th, at about 10 o'clock, a number of men rushed into the Chapel at *St. Ann's Bay*, and violently destroyed the windows, with part of the pews and benches, causing great alarm to the Missionary and his wife, who were residing under the same roof. The next day that Missionary brought this outrage before two of the Magistrates :—Messrs. Thomas Raffington, and William S. Harker, who examined several witnesses, but afforded no adequate protection. In consequence of being left without protection by those who had the Military force under their command, the Missionary, with his wife and infant child, were compelled to flee from their home for safety, and on the following Tuesday, in the forenoon, the whole building, comprising the chapel and residence, was pulled down, and the materials stolen. Among the parties engaged in this act were Dr. George R. Stennett, and Lieut. Henry Cox, jun. (Magistrates) and Capt. Samuel Drake, (Head Constable.)

We are informed that on the last-mentioned day, some Magistrates sent for the boxes of the Missionary to the Court House, searched them, and took out sundry papers, and other of their contents.

On the 24th February, *Ebony Chapel*, at Hayes Savanna, in Vere, was wilfully destroyed by fire. A day or two before, Mr. Hector McLean, Wood, a Magistrate, with another person, went and broke some of the windows of the Chapel, and took away the key.

On Friday, 6th April, about 10 o'clock at night, a mob of *white* men armed with swords, pistols, muskets, and bayonets, went to *Mount Charles Chapel* in St. Andrews. In the way from the gate of the premises to the house, they met with a poor old man (a free negro) unarmed, and fell upon him with their swords, cutting him severely in several places on his head and body, and one of them with a bayonet stabbed him in his side.

When they got to the house they broke open the door, and fired in at it; some of them broke the windows of the bed room, forcing in the glass, frames, and shutters, with such violence, that the bed in which Mrs. Baylis (the Missionary's wife) and her infant were lying, was nearly covered with pieces of glass. They then fired in at each of the windows, and one of the ruffians applied a candle to one side of the room for the purpose of setting it on fire; but the candle was put out. They proceeded to break the hall window, swearing the house should be down that night. Seeing the candle was out, one of them broke open the door of an Out-House, saying he wanted fire, and that he would burn down the house; but the alarm being given, they made off.

The chapels and places of worship at the following stations have also been destroyed, viz:—

Savanna-la-Mar,
Ridgeland, or Fullers Field, } Westmoreland,
Green Island, (a hired house)
Browns Town,
Ocho Rios, (a hired house).

On the 10th January, nine dozens of Madeira Wine, which were being sent from Mr. Burchell's residence in Montego Bay, to him on board the ship Garland Grove, were taken possession of by Lieut. John Henry Morris, and have never since been restored. On the 12th, the same person returned, accompanied by Mr. James Gordon, (a Magistrate) who said, that by " order of Sir Willoughby Cotton, he came to see what quantity of wine was remaining." They went into the store, counted the wine, locked up the store, and took the key away. The key was not returned so late as the 5th of April.

Besides the particular instances mentioned, much more of the private property of the Missionaries has been destroyed or injured, during and since Martial Law.

The loss of property sustained by the Mission, amounts to upwards of £20,000 currency.

The Jamaica Courant (understood to be the newspaper most exten-sively circulated in this island,) has endeavored, and still endeavors, with impunity, to excite the inhabitants to the commission of every species of outrage on the Missionaries, recommending destruction of property, and even threatening life if they remain on the island. This paper is generally (and from the almost universal support it receives, is properly) considered as the organ of the Colony. Coinciding in opinion with the Jamaica Courant and other newspapers, many of the inhabitants' of this island have connected themselves in an Association, under the designation of " The Colonial Church Union ;" the predominant object whereof is to procure the expulsion of all the Missionaries from the island—an endeavor, in fact, to deprive " Englishmen of the right to abide in their own country so long as they please, and not to be driven from it unless by the sentence of the law ;" and they submit, that an Association for such a purpose, is illegal, and at variance with the whole spirit of the British Constitution.

The first place at which this " Union" was set on foot, was St. Ann's Bay, where, on the 15th of February, *after* the demolition of several chapels, and *the promulgation of the Proclamation*, the following, among other resolutions, was passed.—

" Sixth. That it is expected from every Member of the Union, that he will lend his influence and *support on all occasions*, to those patriots who, in behalf of the paramount laws of Society, have hazarded their personal responsibility for our preservation, from the murderous machi-nations of our enemies."

The Presidents of this meeting publicly announced, are the Hon. Henry Cox, *Custos* of St Ann's, Major General in the Militia, and Member of the House of Assembly ; and James Lawrence Hilton, Esq. a Magistrate of that parish, and also a Major General, two of the Authorities who are required by the Proclamation to *prosecute* the offenders, *and prevent further outrages* in that parish.

In Spanish Town, the " Colonial Church Union" for the County of Middlesex, was held on the 21st March—and the resolutions of all the Parochial Meetings seem to have been there recognized and amalgamated.

The Hon. John Lunan, a *Judge* of the Supreme Court of the island, *Custos* of the Precinct of St. Catherine, and Member of Assembly, was appointed President of this Meeting.

It would be an endless undertaking to mention all the Law preservers and Justices of the Peace, who are members of this illegal and peace-disturbing Society; but the Missionaries cannot omit to notice, that the Custodes ·of the several parishes of Trelawney, Manchester, and Vere, have accepted the office of President in their respective parishes. In the parish of Trelawney, one Magistrate, Mr. William Dyer, publishes a newspaper, called " the Cornwall Courier," in which he has repeatedly urged that the Missionaries should be tarred and feathered. An attempt was made on the 7th April, to practise this on the Wesleyan Missionary at Falmouth—and in the next number of that paper, this act was spoken. of with approbation. Our eyes cannot be shut to the fact, that William Dyer, Editor, and William Dyer, Magistrate, are one and the same person; and it seems a little too much to expect from human nature, that what the Editor recommends and applauds, the Magistrate will very rigidly judge, or severely punish.

Another Magistrate, Joseph Hodgson, who resided within a few doors of the place where this disturbance occurred, was applied to for assistance. His reply to the applicant was, that " she had better go home, they would not *hurt* the Minister." These instances of the degree of sanction which some Magistrates give to the acts of violence committed on the Missionaries, were adverted to in a letter addressed to His Excellency's Secretary on the 14th instant.

The following Estimate has been forwarded to the Committee of the Baptist Missionary Society, as the Amount required in order to rebuild, at the lowest possible rate, the Places of Worship destroyed. The Sums are in Jamaica currency.

	£.	s.	d.
Salter's Hill.—Burnt by order of the Captain of Militia, stationed at Latium · value	4000	0	0
Falmouth.—Pulled down by the Saint Ann's Militia, while occupied as Barracks · value	3000	0	0
Montego Bay.—Pulled down at Mid-day by the Inhabitants, headed by several of the Magistrates · · · · · · · · · · · · · · value	6000	0	0
Savannah-la-Mar.—Pulled down by the Parishioners · · · · value	700	0	0
Ridgeland, alias *Fuller's-field.*—Burnt by two Overseers. A valuable House · value	1000	0	0
Rio Bueno.—Burnt · value	1000	0	0
Stewart's Town —Injured to the amount of · · · · · · · · · · · · · · · · · ·	250	0	0
Brown's Town.—Pulled down by the Inhabitants · · · · · · · · value	800	0	0
St. Ann's Bay.—Pulled down by the Inhabitants of the Parish, value	3500	0	0
Ebony Chapel.—Burnt · value	500	0	0
Total Amount of Chapels destroyed· · · · · · · · · ·	20750	0	0
Loss in the destruction of Mission Property, in Houses rented :			
Gurney's Mount.—Pulpit, benches, &c. · · · · · · · · · · · · · · · · · · ·	300	0	0
Putney.—Benches burnt ·	50	0	0
Lucea.—Benches and lamps· ·	50	0	0
Ocho Rios.—Pulpit, pews, and benches · · · · · · · · · · · · · · · · · · ·	100	0	0
	21250	0	0
The Chapel at Lucea, belonging to the General Baptists, but occupied by our Society, pulled down. Offered for Sale by the General Baptist Society for· ·	900	0	0
Losses in horses, furniture, clothes, books, &c. &c. partly belonging to individual Missionaries, and partly to the Society, about	500	0	0
Extra Expenses incurred by travelling, expresses, and Mr. Knibb's passage home · at least	600	0	0
	£23,250	0	0

In the above Statement we have not enumerated the Expense of the Trials, not being certain what the Amount will be.

SECTION II.

Causes of the Insurrection.

In the months of August and September, 1831, Public Meetings were held in many, if not all the parishes throughout the island, the avowed object of which may be learnt from the following Resolutions, unanimously adopted at two of them. At these meetings, slaves as well as others were present, and the proceedings, being inserted in the newspapers, were matters of general notoriety :

" At a very numerous and respectable meeting of the inhabitants of the parish of St. Ann, convened by his honor the Custos, this 6th day of August, 1831, and held at the Court House, St. Ann's Bay, his honor the Custos having been called to the chair, the following resolutions were unanimously agreed to :—

" Resolved—That we, the inhabitants of the parish of St. Ann, have repeatedly expressed our warmest indignation at, and abhorrence of, the oppressive measures pursued by the British Government towards the West India Colonies.

" Resolved—That while there was a hope of conciliating our implacable foes, we acquiesced cheerfully in the conduct of our legislature ; but it is now evident that the concessions yielded by that body, have been successively obtained under pledges and promises on the part of Ministers, ' to abstain from all future interference in our local concerns;' which pledges have been violated in every instance ; giving us thereby convincing proof that perfidy and determined oppression, as far as regards the colonies, are the ruling principles of the British Cabinet.

" Resolved—That hitherto, under the most marked infractions of our rights and privileges, we have been loyal ; the attachment to the mother country has indeed long, very long, outlived her justice ; and it would now be with grief that we should divest ourselves of a feeling, ' which has grown with our growth, and has strengthened with our strength;' but when we see ourselves scorned, betrayed, devoted to ruin and slaughter, delivered over to the enemies of our country, we consider that we are bound by every principle, human and divine, TO RESIST.'

The following are some of the Resolutions of Trelawney :—

" Resolved, that the means devised by a faction in the House of Commons to deprive us of our property, if carried into effect, cannot fail to create a servile war of too horrible a nature to contemplate, and that any person who attempts to produce or promote such war is an enemy to his country."

" Resolved, that the conduct of the British Government in taxing us higher than other subjects ; in fostering our enemies and listening to their falsehoods against us ; in rejecting statements from impartial persons in our favor ; in allowing designing men, under the saintly cloak of religion, not only to pilfer our peasantry of their savings, but also to sow discontent and rebellion amongst them ; in threatening to withdraw troops, for whose protection we have doubly paid, and which we might claim as our right, at a time a servile war may be apprehended; is most heartless, and in violation of justice, humanity, and sound policy."

The resolutions proceed to state, that " thrown" as they are about to be, " as a prey before misguided savages, we have no other alternative than to resist ;" and to pray the King " that we may be absolved from our allegiance, and allowed to seek that protection from another nation which is so unjustly and cruelly withheld from us by our own."

Subsequently to the honourable acquittal of Mr. Knibb, he was requested by the Hon. the Chief Justice, and W. Miller, Esq. late Custos of Trelawney, to use his exertions to discover the mode in which the insurrection was planned. To facilitate the enquiry, a promise was made to two of the principal prisoners, styled Colonel Gardner and Captain Dove, that their lives should be spared if they made a full confession.

The following is the confession of these men, as taken down in the gaol by Mr. Knibb:—

They both stated, that they first heard about freedom from the negroes about Belvidere and Retrieve, but that they did not put any belief in it, and Gardner said, that he used his efforts to make the people think that it was not so.

Though they had heard much talk about it, they both solemnly denied having any connexion with the plot until Christmas-day. When, after morning prayers at the Baptist Chapel at Montego Bay, they went down the street, and met Guthrie, Sharp, George Taylor, and others, members of the Church, who were talking about the freedom of the slaves? George Taylor was strongly advising Sharp not to refuse to go to work after Christmas, as it would bring a disgrace upon the gospel. Sharp said, what is then to become of the oath we have taken in the country? We then went to the Chapel, and saw Thomas Williams, a Deacon in the Church. Gardner says, he strongly advised us to go to our work after Christmas, saying, if freedom is come, we shall get it quietly, but if they did what was wrong it would bring a disgrace upon Religion. Sharp said, I know we are *free*, I have read it in the English papers—I have taken an *oath* not to work after Christmas, without some satisfaction, and I will *not*. He then left us.

Gardner stated, that he then went in the street to buy grass for his horse, and on his way he met Guthrie, who asked him to take second breakfast with him after Chapel, which he promised to do. Went to Chapel, and heard Mr. Gardner preach,—his preaching make him stagger, and think freedom *not* come. So he make up his mind to go to work whatever others did. After Chapel went up to Cunningham's Hill, and on the way up met Dove. Guthrie said, Well, Dove, I hope you will not be hurt at my not asking you to the Hill, I intended to do it, but will you come? Dove said, yes, I am not offended, I will go with you.

At this meeting James Gardner, Thomas Gooden, William James, Charles Campbell, ourselves, and Guthrie, were present. When we entered the house, Guthrie said, Well, gentlemen, I am glad to see you, I have spirits and wine, what will you take to drink? We all chose wine. Guthrie poured it out, and taking his glass, said, Well, friends, I hope the time will soon come when we shall have our privilege, and when we shall drink our wine free. I hope we shall soon have Little Breeches under our feet. They all drank. Gardner says, I asked what this Little Breeches heard—Guthrie say he is my master. Mr. Grignon and I hear him say, that the king is going to give us free, but he hoped all his friends will be of his mind, and spill their blood first. But I'll be the first to do the job, though I am his slave. I'll give him a pill, snapping his fingers, as I follow him. Before we left, Guthrie introduced a young woman to us, and said, This is to be Mrs. Guthrie, after all is over.

We both left together, and went home. When I, Gardner, got to Greenwich, the people asked me what they were to do after the holidays. I said, I shall go to work, for I do not believe that the free paper has come. They said, No, we will not go to work, we believe the king has made us free. I then said, Well, if you will not believe me, I cannot tell. Get your breakfast, and go and sit down in the king's road; hurt no one, and ask Buckra whether free come or not, when he passes. While I was sitting in my house, on Tuesday night, some one knocked at the door. When I open the door, I saw Campbell from Retrieve, who said, Won't you come with us? I said for what? He said, to *fight for freedom*. I said, No, it is a bad thing. On looking out I saw a number of men, armed with guns and swords. They appointed to meet at Haslymph next evening, and I went with Dove; a great many were there, but cannot tell how many, as it was very dark. After much talk, they could not agree what to do, when one set fire to Haslymph's trash-house; when it burn, they all fire their guns, and blow their conks. I went home, as I did not like to see the places fired.—Both of us were present at the attack made upon Mr. Grignon, and the soldiers at the Montpelliers. Dove had a pistol, it was loaded, but he did not fire it; he was frightened at the bullets, and went under the wall. Charles Campbell was commander, and told those who had not any guns to keep back. Campbell led his company along the king's road, and Johnstone led his company by the negro houses as ambush. Johnstone was killed on the spot, and so near the white people that they could not carry him away. Campbell was shot through the body. They took him to Gardner's house, at Greenwich, and sent for Gardner, who had gone into a grass piece. We both went to see him, but he could not speak. He died in the morning —we made a rough coffin, and buried him. Gardner read the burial service over him. Dove declares that he never left the property to fight after this battle.

In answer to my questions, as to what made them believe that the free paper had come, they stated that they all put much confidence in Sharp, who told them he had seen it in the papers, and who sent Edward Ramsey round to all the properties to tell the people it was so.

Gardner stated, that John Morris, from Duckett's came to Greenwich, and said that he had one pistol, and that he had given three guns to his people; that he had taken three more guns, and four pistols from Mr. G. Hale's mountain, and when I told him that I did not think it true that the king had made us free, he said, that he was sure that it was true, for when the women with pickaniny at Duckett's, go to master Grignon at Christmas for allowance, master say, that they must now look to their friends in England for allowance, for he had no more to give them. John Morris argued long on this, and say, If we not free, what make master Grignon say so? This make all the people get stout upon it, and they throw down their hoe, and say, *they are free.*

Parties of the rebels with guns often came to me at Greenwich, but not liking the burnings I hid from them. One night John Morris, and Thomas Horton, from Shuttlewood Cave, met more than 100 men armed. I went to the top of a hill, that they might not know where I was. Thinking that they were gone, I came down in the morning, when I found them drawn up like soldiers, and they make me go with them to Argyle. We went through Chester Castle. When we came there Ricketts from Chester Castle began to chop Agnus M'Can with his sword, over the shoulder. I would not allow him, and prevented him from killing him. This man is yet alive, and can prove what I say. I then stopped them from beating M'Can's mother Do not know who it was that burnt the property. John Morris and Thomas Horton were in command. Went home and felt vexed that the people burn the properties; never thought that they would do so, but that all would sit still and see whether the free paper come or not.

Dove stated that James Heulier, from Belvidera, was a chief man among the rebels—he had been a runaway for five years.

Edward Ramsey told us and the people, that he had often heard his master say, that negro was to be free after Christmas. This was at Cow Park. He was captain of a company.

Bailey, a yellow skin negro belonging to Miss Williams, read the paper about freedom to the people in the country, and told them that it came from England. He was a captain,—saw him and heard him tell the people to fight.

John Thorp Lawrence, *alias* Daddy Tharp, he is not praying at all—was a great horseman, pulled down Little Bridge, he attacked the white people at Long Hill, told me (Gardner) that white man at Lethe gave him his gun and pistol, and told him how to make cartridges, and that he did right to fight for freedom. After they had answered a number of other questions, which I do not think it necessary to record, I asked them the following questions: Whether they had ever heard any minister tell them that they were free, or whether the negroes said, that Mr. Burchell had gone home to fetch free paper for them? They both said, Minister, we feel for you and Mr. Burchell, and the other ministers; you left your mother to teach we, and now when negro do wrong, they put it on you. We have often been asked the question, but if we are to die for it, you never did tell us. Black men ruin us. Gardner said, I know you, minister. I have been a member of the Church for eight years, and never been reproved for a fault either by minister or overseer. Mr. Burchell baptize me the first, in the river, but my character is now gone, I am a ruined man, and I would tell of any, even if it my mother, if they had deceived me; but if I die for it I will not tell a lie upon Mr. Burchell.

Poor man, I feel for him, had I followed his advice I should not have been in this trouble. Wicked men and a wicked heart led me into it. I urged them to say if they had ever heard a minister say a word about freedom. They said *No,* they never did. They both said that they had never heard the leaders in the rebellion say, it was Mr. B. or that he had gone home to fetch free paper. It was the unguarded expressions of the overseers, and the (news) papers.

Edward Hilton, another prisoner, stated that he was at Retrieve Estate, about two months before Christmas, where he met Samuel Sharp and others :—

Hilton asked, Let me know what we came for. Sharp said that he understood by the newspapers that the king had made them free, and that the white people, and Grignon especially, make assembly at Mr. Watt and the Court House, making a studyation to destroy all the black men, and leave all the women. That they would put them before the muzzles of their guns and shoot them like pigeons. He, Hilton, said, that if they came to take life for nothing he would run for it, but negro is not to be trusted. If one negro swear false he might hang a thousand, and get himself free for it. But if he Sharp swear it, then he would believe him. Sharp said, in the 15th chapter of Matthew, it says, " Swear not at all neither by heaven, for 'tis God's throne, nor by the earth, for 'tis God's footstool, nor by Jerusalem, for 'tis the city of the Great King, nor by your head, because you cannot make one hair white or black," so must take word of mouth, or else you make him a liar. The king is going to send 5000 black soldiers to guard the country. After more discourse had a prayer, then went home. Next Sunday not preaching day at Montego Bay, so went to Lamb's house and saw Thomas Reid, and asked him if he knew about this meeting kept by Sharp at Retrieve. He said yes, but he had never been there. Said that Sharp had sent for him to hear it. But Reid must not have any thing to do with it. Tell him not to trust a negro, for one could get a thousand hanged. Thomas Reid is yet alive, and can prove the discourse.

Four weeks before Christmas went to Duckett's Spring, and stopped at John Morris's house. Morris was asleep; William White came in and shook him, so that he might get awake. When he awoke he told him that he wanted him to go to the meeting. They went out, and he (Hilton) went with them. Saw John Sharp, of Catadupa, Alexander from Richmond Hill, and Sam Sharp's father-in-law, present. John Sharp asked Morris if he knew what he was come about. Morris said no; I want to see every body on the property. Morris said it is too late, they have taken prayers and gone home. John Sharp then said that he had come to put every person to his oath that they were not to go to work after Christmas. They took a Bible, and swore to that effect. After that they eat supper, and went away. Has heard that the meetings at Retrieve were held very often, but did not go back because he was afraid to meet the negroes.

Heard no more about it till Christmas morning, when he came down to the Chapel at Montego Bay. After 7 o'clock, morning prayer, Sam Sharp came to me and said, Minister is going to take all the members together, and if he ask you any thing about freedom, or whether you intend to work after Christmas, tell him No,—that you know very well that you are free, and that you won't work again for any body unless you get paid for it. Minister did not call us, but Samuel Vaughan speak to a few of us, and told us to behave ourselves during the Christmas; that we must not get drunk lest we fall into temptation, and that prayer was the way to heaven. After meeting had closed, went to Richard Bailey, at the Long Stores; saw James Gardner and William James from Duckett's Spring there. We took second breakfast. When we had sat down, Bailey looked for an old newspaper, and said, This is not the right one; this is four months old, and this tells us that eight years back, women were not to get any flogging. I then left the house about some business, and soon came back again; when Richard Bailey said he had found the other paper under his bed; recollects that he said that the paper said, that the English people will not submit under the *brutish custom anv longer.* A paper was produced, which Hilton said was the same, he knew it by the ship on the top.* Thomas Reid told me that Edward Ramsey came to Lamb's River to put oath to all the people, but that he objected to it.

Went to Mountain after the Tuesday; was down at the Bay; saw the fire on Tuesday night, and heard the shells blow at Haslymph. Saw Gardner at Cow Park, in the road. He had no crew; did not see him give any orders. Edward Barrett was there with a gun, and they called him captain; has always heard from Cuffee, who is in jail, that Sharp swear all the people at Haslymph. Asked Thomas Williams, a leader on the Bay, whether it be true what was saying about freedom. He told me No; that foolish people put it in their heads. He is sure he never heard Mr. Burchell say a word about it; never heard negro say that Mr. Burchell had gone to bring their freedom. But they make it all up at Retrieve.

John Sharp, (the individual who planned the whole)—

After much trouble, and an evident desire not to say more than he could help, he stated that several weeks before Christmas, they met at a house at Retrieve, *and confirmed* what Hilton had said. It was at this place that they first planned that they would not work after Christmas. It was thus done. A Bible was brought and put on the table. He then got up and said, If ever I witness any thing against my brother and sister, concerning this matter, may hell be my portion! Nobody was present from Montego Bay: Dove and Gardner were not there.

Met two weeks before Christmas, it was *not a religious meeting*. But the drivers on different properties met to consult what to do. Some said, in answer to the question, What is to be done when we go to take order after Christmas? We will go and take it, and fire the whip, but none are to come out to work—this we will explain to the people. When all had done, Johnstone of Retrieve get up and say, This will not do, for the women are chicken hearted, and if they see the driver in the field, some will get frightened and go, and spoil all. I say, when the Busha send for me I will give the order, but I will not go out. When Busha hear this, and send for me, I will say, the people know well that they are free, and will not work any more without some satisfaction. Now by the time I say this, Busha will be ordering his horse to go to the Bay, to say that we rebel. Then we won't let him go, but will take away his horse and his gun, and will say to him, Busha, we don't rebel, but we won't work without some satisfaction. We work long enough for nothing.

Never heard of any agreement to burn any properties; all we swear was, that as we know that we are free, we will not work for Buckra unless he pay us for it.

In trying to discover what made them think that they were free, they said the papers, and Busha common-talk. Sharp said that Edward Ramsey told him, that his master told him that freedom was come from England, but that he would shoot every d——d black rascal before they should get it.

Such is the earnest desire of the negroes to know what is going on in England, that it is a common practice for the pedlars, who go about from one estate to another with trinkets, &c. for sale, to take newspapers with them, by reading which they soon collect a number of customers around them.

---

* A number of the Falmouth Packet.

SECTION III.

Conduct and Sentiments of the Colonists towards the British Government and the Sectarians.

It seems requisite, under this head, to shew, by a few examples, the character of the public Press in Jamaica.

The *Jamaica Courant*, Feb. 10, contains the following:—

Extract of a Letter from an Officer of the St. Ann's Western Regiment, to the Editor, dated 7th Feb, 1832.

" Our primary ardour has been unabated. We have never allowed these deluded wretches time to rest; night and day have we been at them, and have made terrible slaughter among them. And now, at the end of a six weeks' campaign, we are neglected—not thought of, because the Governor must have a little fun with Tom Hill and his yacht. The few wretches who are now out, are hiding in the cane-pieces, and we occasionally get a bullet or two at them. On Sunday morning, five were shot, who were fallen in with and attempted to escape. I shall not consider that we are safe, although all this havoc has been made among the rebels; although they may have now found the inutility of opposing the strong force which can be opposed to them, until we can fall upon some plan of getting rid of the infernal race of Baptists, which we have so long fostered in our bosoms, and of demolishing their bloody pandemoniums."

Extract of a letter, dated Falmouth, Feb. 7, 9 o'clock, p. m. :—

" I cannot allow the post to start, without saying that I have remained long enough at Falmouth to see the Baptist and Methodist Chapels pulled down. This good work was accomplished this day, by the troops after their return—conquerors from the seat of war. Lots of groans as you may imagine, from the Saints and their followers. It is impossible for me to give you a description of the appearance of our brave Militia men on their arrival in this town. The poor fellows cut a miserable appearance; you could not actually tell whether they were black, white, yellow, or any other color."

Extract of another letter of the same date :—

" Let Bruce know that the great and glorious work has commenced. It is now 10 o'clock, and all hands at work, demolishing the Baptist and Wesleyan Chapels. The Methodist Chapel is down, and the men are hard at work at the Baptists'. The roof of the latter is not yet off, but so much injured, as to make it as well off as on. It is standing, true, but supported by a few posts only. The men have gone for fire hooks to complete the work they have undertaken. There is the devil to pay here to-day (as you may suppose) among the Saints and their followers.—Weeping and wailing, and gnashing of teeth—wringing of hands, and groans, interrupted at times, with curses and imprecations on the soldiers."

Half-past 11, Tuesday night, Feb. 7.

" I write in the hopes of this reaching you through the way-bag, as the Post Office has long since been shut. Some true-hearted Jamaicans have truly ennobled themselves this night, by razing to the earth that pestilential hole, Knibbs's Preaching Shop. Verily, friend, they have not spared Box's also. He no more will be able to beat the roll-call to prayers, nor the tatoo upon the consciences of the subscribers of macs—our poor deluded slaves. In plain English, not one stone has been left standing—nay, not even the corner one; and I hope that this goodly example will be followed from Negril to Morant."

Extract of a letter to the Editor, dated Falmouth, 10 o'clock, p. m. 7 Feb. 1832:—

" I trust there will be no occasion for apology in a stranger addressing you, as no doubt you will feel the same pleasure in perusing this as I did in witnessing the act which forms the subject of my communication.

" There is no longer a hive for the drones; the bees have beat them away, and destroyed their hives; no longer have they a shelter to collect maccaronies in, and away they must go.—With what pleasure did I witness the conduct of the brave and intrepid men of the St. Ann's Regiment, while performing that which ought to have been done by the Trelawney Regiment—demolishing the Baptist and Methodist Chapels. This work commenced at eight o'clock, and is still going on; by morning there will not be a stone left standing. I trust the example thus set in Trelawney, will be followed throughout the island; with this difference, that the inhabitants of every parish will do their own duty, and not require others to perform it. It was highly amusing to see the " *Cobblers*," flocks in the streets, groaning and wondering where their *preachers* would now get money to build other Chapels."

Again, Feb. 18, the Editor states that he had been present at the Methodist Chapel on the Parade, Kingston, and heard one of the ministers, whom he styles "a stout consecrated cobbler," lecture thirteen men because they had not performed their duty fearlessly, during the late rebellion. On this he proceeds to remark as follows: —

" Is it come to this, that when the danger is supposed to be over, that the preachers of all denominations, who found it *prudent* to quit the country, should assemble in Kingston, and pretend to be instructors of each other, and point out how they are *in future to conduct themselves?* Their treason to the country has been discovered, and by a show of about thirty vagabond preachers, who dare not show their *noses* out of Kingston, they are endeavoring to excite a sympathy for their sufferings ! The time has passed, and their conduct is now understood, and none but those who encourage rebellion would, for one moment, countenance the conduct they are pursuing. If they are really the servants of the Lord Jesus, what have they to be afraid of? Their master performed many miracles, but alas! he was crucified—a consummation which we devoutly pray his pretended servants may experience ; and as we intend shortly to publish an almanack, we shall be very happy to canonize these gentry, by placing their names as Saints, in *black letter*. Now for the oration. The *Rev.* bawler addressed his thirteen culprits, and asked them if *their* mission was not one of peace? The poor d—-ls, of course, nodded assent. He then remarked, with a degree of energy which we are sorry was not exerted in a good cause—*Are* you not ambassadors from God? Another nod! Then said the preacher, *persevere*—here he made a pause of a few seconds, and then told the *criminals again* to persevere in maintaining peace and good order ! ! ! ! These men are very kind, and no doubt *preach peace* on earth, and good will towards all men ! The dear *babes*, how we love them ! Merely because we know they love *us ! !* We are however not bigots, either in politics or religion, and if they could point out the same number of *good* men among them which would have saved Sodom and Gomorrah, we would like Lot " *beg for them*," but as we know that such a number could not be found, we hope they may be *ordered* to " march" at a moment's warning, without sustaining a loss equal to that which poor Lot experienced."

Cornwall Courier, Feb. 15.—

" Since our last we have received accounts of the destruction of every one of those pandemoniums of insurrection and rebellion, the Baptist preaching shops, from Savanna-la-Mar to Brown's Town, in St. Ann's. They have been destroyed partly by the Militia and partly by some of their own followers, who have had their eyes opened by recent events, which have taught them that the Baptist Parsons were not the Sovereigns of Jamaica. Several of the Wesleyan Chapels have also been either totally or partially destroyed ; a fit but trifling retribution for the loss these men have caused to the proprietors of those estates that have been burnt by the incendiaries, who were instigated to commit the crimes, for which so many of them have suffered, by these preachers.—We can only say in the words of the Reformer, John Knox—" To get rid of the Rooks effectually, you must destroy their nests."—As to the rooks—the preachers—we would recommend the advice of our staunch friend, James M'Queen, to be observed towards them :—" Tar and feather them wherever you meet them," and drive them off the island, excepting always those who may merit a greater elevation—a more exalted distinction.

Cornwall Courier, Feb. 22.—

" The war may now be considered at an end; the deluded victims of Sectarian treachery have tried their strength, and are satisfied of their utter incapacity for warlike operations. The ease and celerity with which they have been subdued, and appalling examples, have struck a terror which will not be got the better of; and we might anticipate a long series of peace, were it not for the portentous events with which the political horizon of the parent state is overcharged. There, we are to expect nothing but what the most rancorous animosity, backed by power, may inflict; but we are happy to observe that a feeling and spirit is aroused throughout the island, which will enable the injured and insulted inhabitants to withstand and repel the assaults of their enemies.—This has been manifested in the destruction of those dens of sedition and hypocrisy—the Sectarian Chapels. It is a measure of just retribution for that devastation which was inflicted on unoffending individuals, by the base and cowardly arts of those *authorised** traitors; the indignation of the community had been sufficiently inflamed, by the dissension which their doctrines had sown between the master and the slave. It wanted but this to fill up the measure of their iniquity, for bringing upon them deserved vengeance. It has fallen—and fallen, justly, on those who are ' the head and front of the offending.'—If any man doubts this, let him look at the confessions of those victims who have expiated their crimes on the scaffold; let him look to the examinations on the pending trials of Burchell, Knibb, and Gardner. These would be sufficient to convict the Sectarians, even before their own corrupt tribunals: but we are too well aware of the weakness of our courts of law, to suppose that they will meet the fate they so justly merit, nor have we any thing to expect from an application to the Legislature; for although the popular part might willingly pass an act to root them out from the soil, yet we know, but too well, that it is an injunction imperatively laid by Ministers on the Governor, to encourage and support these incendiaries by every means in his power.

Some there are who aver that it might have been better to await such an application to the House of Assembly; we beg leave to answer—that with this conviction before us, no benefit whatever could have followed.—We say, that no redress awaits our deeply seated injuries from Law, Legislation, or Government. Retribution has been inflicted in the most speedy manner, and it has been inflicted by those who had a full right to 'do so. Society has its rights—as well as Legislature. The prerogative of Society is undeniable; it is at all times greater than that of legislature, which is dependent on it.—Here is one of those instances where the representatives were powerless, and the people have taken it in their own hands. When we say the people, we do not mean a mob—a gang of thieves and pickpockets, such as the happy politics of England now acknowledge as their liege Lords—but we mean the Magistrates, Vestrymen, and Freeholders of the island, who have been in arms to preserve their property, and who have, *in open day, done this thing in self-defence!*

The COLONIAL CHURCH UNION, established in St. Ann's, works well, and gives an assurance that the leading men of the country are zealously performing their duty; and, as an advanced guard, are diligently protecting our interests.— counteracting and exposing the machinations of our enemies. We trust that every man in the island will enrol his name in this Society; there is an absolute necessity for a combination of this kind, throughout every parish. We refer, for this purpose, to the repeated admonitions of those able journalists who have advocated our cause in the Mother-Country; they tell us, that nothing but a firm, decided, and general Union, can shield us from the frantic schemes of our enemies, or the tyrannical measures of their obsequious SLAVES—the Ministers of the Crown!

The result of the rebellion has been, to open the eyes of the community to the utter incapacity of our laboring class as combatants, and has completely dispelled

* Authorised by Government.

that idle panic which pervaded the island, on account of their vast apparent numerical strength. This bubble has burst, but we must prepare for other contests. —The very defence of our lives and properties will be construed by the Anti-Colonists, into a crime of the deepest dye. They will rave for the unexpected failure of their insurrectionary plans, and a crusade will be preached up against us, and permitted by Government. The *revolutionary Parliament of England*, *will emulate the revolutionary Parliament of Robespierre*; and we call on every man throughout the island to say,—whether he would not rather die with arms in his hand, than submit to such an unjust, unprincipled, act of tyranny?

This is what Jamaica has to expect.—This is what your Agent, Mr. Burge, has warned you will come to pass. The present Administration has told you, you have nothing to hope from them.—The reformed Administration will complete your ruin, unless the Colonists preserve that tone and spirit of resistance, which can alone bear them through the portending storm.

Jamaica Courant, Feb, 29.—Extract of a Letter by " Conservator," to the House of Assembly :—

The orders in council lately proclaimed in the unfortunate Crown colonies, will no doubt be laid before you. Gentlemen, you cannot have already forgotten the threat of that presumptuous impotent half-fledged stripling, Lord Howick, made in Parliament, that he would compel you to adopt them without the alteration of a word, or even a letter!!

If for one moment you entertain that document, coupled with such a threat— in the next, resign the trust which your constituents have reposed in you.

No, hang or burn, if you will, the puppet's effigy with the orders crammed in the throat, under the gallows, if there is such a thing in the good town of Saint Jago de la Vega; but pray do not let them disgrace your mace, by laying on the same table with it.

Jamaica Courant, March 1.—

On an attentive re-perusal of the Governor's opening speech to the Legislature, we are sorry to remark that his Excellency persists, in his allusions to " the machinations which have been employed to seduce the slaves into rebellion," to talk of their " *allegiance!!* and the *duty* they owe to their masters. The Earl of Belmore has been long enough in Jamaica to know that the slaves owe no *allegiance*, and that the contract between their owners and the Government of the Mother Country provides only for their *obedience* to their masters ; and we deprecate the idea of inculcating upon the negro mind the bare supposition that the King has any control whatever over him : and we have no doubt that to the frequency with which such doctrines have been held out by the Sectarians, is mainly to be attributed the cause of the late rebellion.

We had intended to add several Extracts illustrative of the formation and objects of the " Colonial Church Union," formed for the avowed purpose of expelling Sectarianism from the island, but must confine ourselves to the following, taken from the *Courant* of March 3, which clearly shews what is meant by " Sectarianism," since it complains that it has flourished even among the members of our own (the Established] Church!

The Colonial Church Union.

This auspicious measure flourishes—eleven parishes are already organized within its combining influence—and an active principle of life and energy is already infused into our hitherto lifeless body, which will soon circulate through every vein of the Colony, and give an impulse to its struggles, which nothing can withstand— nothing, at least, which can be brought against it in the present dislocated state of affairs in the parent isle—for in such a cruel situation are we placed, that all we have to guard against is the unnatural conduct of our own misguided parent! In less than four months have we to dread the infuriated exertions of our enemies,—

the whole battery of the Colonial Office will then be opened against us, aided by the small arms, the rifles, of those assassin brigands, the Sectarians, who are so expert in picking off our best men, the victims of treachery and revenge. For this we must be prepared by our Unions, as well as against the harassing prosecutions which will be instituted, but which need not be feared, so long as the Jury Box be within its range. The plan is understood to be this, and it is time it should be widely promulgated:—The Parochial Unions are to become sub-committees to one *Grand Island* Union, which will be directed by an acting committee of two or more members of each of the parochial committees, headed by a President, to be elected by the *general voice of the members,* with Secretaries and an Island Treasurer, to meet where, and as often as occasion may require. The first general meeting will shortly be convened, when such provisions, and rules, and *orders,* will be promulgated, as will anticipate the dreaded blow, and organize the Country against the future interference of those who have rendered such strong measures necessary. Above all things, care must be taken to exclude, and narrowly to watch the conduct of *suspected persons, of which many are amongst us,* whom it is now necessary to hold up to public shame and reproach. The existence of the Union, as an effective body, requires *their* exposure, and its members will bear harmless the man who dares to bring such forward. They will also protect all those who, for the *general good,* are active in expelling from our veins the poison of Sectarianism, and preventing its further infusion; and one of their first and strongest efforts should be to destroy those organs of sedition and blasphemy, which have assisted in disseminating that poison:—to support, or countenance, in short, *no press or person that shall advocate the hateful cause of the Dissenters!* and to petition the Assembly to place *our own Clergy* under the control of *our own people,* and their representatives *in Vestry,* even to the expulsion of those missionaries and curates, who are still here paid by, and under the influence of our enemies; and who have already been detected in their vile vocation. The old Church government and discipline was better than the present—*let then the old laws revive.* The Episcopal Government has here been an experiment, which has failed; for under it, sectarianism has increased ten-fold, and flourished even amongst the ministers of our own church. In fact, sectarianism came in with that system;—*let them expire together.* We have lately seen the danger of trusting our people to the instruction of those who are not under our own control; let us, therefore, henceforward hold the purse and power in our own hands, and let every member of the Colonial Church Union think, that, as in battle, the field may be won by his own arm, so in the present.

The means taken to procure evidence condemning the Missionaries have already been partially made known to the public.

The following confession of Samuel Stennett, the witness against Mr. Burchell, was made before John Manderson and T. Raeburn, Esqrs. of Montego Bay:—

Jamaica—Personally appeared before me Samuel Stennett, of the Parish of St. James, county of Cornwall, and island aforesaid being duly sworn, maketh oath and saith, That the affidavit made by him against the Baptist Missionaries, T. Burchell, and F. Gardner, which led to their confinement in gaol, was false and unjust; that he never heard from them such facts as he, the deponent, hath sworn against them. That he was instigated to do so by Messrs. George Delisser, George McFarquhar Lawson, jun., Joseph Bowen, and W. C. Morris, the former of whom assured him that he would be well looked upon by the gentlemen of this place, that the country would give him £10 per annum, and that he, George Delisser, would make it £50. This deponent further saith, that he is induced to make this declaration to relieve his conscience, as he knew nothing against the said Missionaries, and that he never joined the Baptist Society as a member until after Mr. Burchell had left the country. So help me God.

Lewis Williams, a free black man of Falmouth,

Saw an old man from Windsor Lodge hanged—when they tie him and bring him down, he said, " Well, I am going to be hanged. Mr. Buchanan, you force Dempshire to tell a lie upon me. Never mind, Sir, God bless you, I hope you may live long. I never told the people any thing about free paper, or to burn the property." Several of the members told me that the old man never told them any thing about freedom. Really believe him a very good old man, have known him four years. Heard Captain Stainby ask a man from Windsor Lodge, when he was going to be hung, Whether the Baptist Parson did not tell you go to free? *No.* Join no Church—Never go to any. Have seen nine hung, do not know names ; but all were asked whether the Baptist Parson did not tell them they *were* free ; all said, *No,* the Parson never tell me any thing of the kind.

Richard Brown, of the same town, who by his industry had been enabled to purchase his own freedom and that of his wife, states that he—

Was present when Robert Hall was led out to be shot at Falmouth; was sentinel. Saw Mr. Jobson and Mr. Russell present. Heard Robert Hall say, that he did not belong to any Church, was christened in the Church of England. Heard Mr. Russell ask him what parson told him he was going to be free? Heard Robert Hall say he never heard parson say so. Heard Mr. Russell say, What, no parson? Answered *No.* Heard Mr. Russell say,—Say Parson Knibb, you Sir. Heard prisoner say, Master, I cannot go tell a lie, I never hear it. Saw the prisoner tied to be shot. Heard Mr. Russell say, Move away that man, (meaning me.) Heard the prisoner say, Me never hear it from minister myself; but the people da go pray, say we going to be free. Does not know what question was put to the prisoner as he was removed.

Was present as sentinel when ——— Bell, from Dromilly, was led out to be shot. Mr. Russell and Mr. Jobson were with him. Heard Mr. Jobson ask him, the prisoner, what he had to say. Prisoner said he had nothing to say, only that he tried to save his master's property, and that the negoes tell a lie upon him. Heard Mr. Russell say to the prisoner, What Church do you go to? Prisoner said, Sometimes go to Chapel. Heard Russell ask prisoner what minister told him he was to be free? Heard prisoner say, No minister tell me so ; it was lie his master's negroes tell upon him. Heard Russell and Jobson say, This man won't tell the truth, being he saw me there, I being one of the brothers in the Church. Saw them take the man away to be shot. Does not know what he or they said, but when Mr. Smith came back, he shook his sword in my face.

Notes of an interview with Venture and Paris, two of the evidences for the crown against Mr. Knibb, made at their earnest request—

Venture, the Baptist leader came to me one day, when I went to the jail, and with tears in his eyes, begged me to speak with him as he had something to tell me ; I told him that I could not, that he was a witness against me, and that I wished him to say all against me that he knew. After the trial I saw him and Paris, when he stated as follows: That Joseph Erskine, the chief witness against me was never at Crooked Spring Chapel but once in his life; that he was in no manner connected with the Church, and that he did not even know me ; that he was among the rebels, and was taken in the woods by the Maroons, when he said, that if they would spare his life, he would tell them all about the parson.

He then told Busha that I and Paris were the leaders on Lima, and we were then taken and put in confine in the stocks at Latimer. Mr. Gunn came and wished to take me out and shoot me, but Busha would not let him. They then said that I kill the sheep at Dumfries, which was not true. When I was brought down to the Bay, I was taken into a private room in the Court House, by young Dr. Lawson. He ask me, What was the oath Mr. Knibb gave the people? When it was that Mr. Knibb told them to burn their masters' properties? What time Mr. Knibb tell them Parson Burchell would be back from England? Whether Mr. Knibb did not tell them that Parson Burchell had gone home to fetch the free paper? Paris said, that the same questions were put to him. They both said No; he never tell us any thing of the kind; he tell us to be obedient to our masters, and to be sure to go to work after Christmas. Venture said, he (Mr. K.) took me aside at Salter's Hill, and speak to him privately to be sure to tell the people to go to their work after Christmas, and not to believe any thing about freedom. We were both then tied and sent to jail.

Had oath given us at the Court House the other day, and were sent to the Grand Jury. They asked me (Venture) about Mr. Knibb, and I told them the same as I said to young Dr. Lawson. They then feel my head and say, Knibb has sworn you not to speak the truth. I say No. I never take oath before to-day, and is now on my oath on the Bible, and is speaking the truth. I cannot tell a lie, minister never did tell me any thing about freedom. They then tell me I is a damn Baptist liar, and will not speak the truth. No other witness present.

Paris said the same, and informed me that Adam would not tell a lie upon me.

SECTION IV.

Conduct of the Missionaries and Religious Slaves during the Insurrection.

UNDER this head we insert a Letter from Samuel M. Barrett, Esq. to Mr. Knibb, dated Cornwall, Feb. 23, and a condensed Statement of Facts, as furnished by Mr. Knibb himself.

Mr. Barrett's Letter is as follows:

Dear Sir—I avail myself of the return of your Messenger to Montego Bay, to express to you the sincere pleasure I feel in hearing of your release from the restraint which had been imposed upon you and your brethren. I can assure you, that I never from the beginning, nor do I at this time, attribute to yourself or to Mr. Burchell, any blame as directly producing or promoting the late melancholy disturbance. Having this feeling, I deeply regret that the feelings of the country should so strongly mark yourself and the other Baptist Ministers out as objects of persecution. My opinion, an opinion resulting from my own frequent and confidential intercourse, not only with my own negroes, but with the negroes of various other estates, is, that religion had nothing to do with the late disturbances; but, on the contrary, its absence was a chief cause of them. No people could have conducted themselves better than all the negroes upon Cambridge and Oxford Estates, and in like manner, the people upon Retreat Pen. Even at the period when the prejudice ran strongest against you, and when it was scarcely politic for a negro to say any thing in your favor, I have, upon every occasion, when I have enquired from any of the members of your congregation upon any of my properties, whether you had ever *taught them to expect freedom*, the answer has invariably been such as to convince me the charges against you were ill-founded. In the absence of all proof to criminate any one in particular, or any class of persons, professional or otherwise, I would not in charity suspect any one, or venture to assign any cause for so great an evil as it has pleased Providence to afflict us with. I should have deeply deplored, for the sake of religion, had any of its Ministers so far perverted the truths of the Gospel, as to create this shedding of blood. I do, therefore, most sincerely rejoice that you stand innocent of all guilt as connected with the late disturbances, so far as any proof has, as yet, been adduced.

I remain, dear Sir,
Your obedient servant,
SAML. M. BARRETT.

Mr. Knibb's Account is:—

Robert Gentle, a leader in Mr. Cantlow's Church, took up Dehany and two other of the rebels.

Huie Barnett, an enquirer, belonging to Falmouth Church, took up Robert Whitter, one of the chief rebels on Pantrepant Estate.

Green Park negroes were celebrated in the papers of the Colony for their good conduct. On that property I had thirty-seven members; the enquirers are double the number. Some of my members on that property took up two rebels who came to set fire to the estate. They came to me to ask me if they had done right, and I assured them they had. A sum of money has been voted to them by the House of Assembly.

They thus conclude a letter written to their mistress, and sent open for my perusal.

" We have been faithful servants of yours, these several years, and hope to continue so, by being enlightened by the gospel. During the rebellion the attorney left the property, the overseer and book-keepers were on guard in the town and country, and we remained steadily, and protected the property to the last, knowing the estate was in danger of being consumed with fire. We therefore trust, mistress, that you will, as a pious soul, unite with us, your slaves, to let our minister remain with us, and aid and assist in defending the gospel of Christ in Jamaica.

JOSEPH HENRY. X
LEWIS WINWRIGHT. X
LEWIS ATHERTON. X
JAMES CAMERON. X"

Charles Campbell, belonging to Weston Favel Estate, a deacon at Falmouth, saved the property, and has received his freedom in consequence.

Edward Barrett, belonging to Oxford, guarded, with the people, the property for a month. We have eighty-six members on this property. He is a deacon of the church at Falmouth.

George Prince of Wales, a member of the church at Falmouth, had the whole charge of the property, the keys of the store, &c. &c. put into his hands, for a month. We have thirty-six members on this estate.

The members of the church at Carlton Estate saved the property, as the following note, from Mrs. Waddell, the wife of a Presbyterian Missionary, will testify. "I am happy to say that some of your people, in this quarter, have adorned the gospel by their becoming conduct, particularly Reeves, Hall, and Gordon." Mr. Cron (the attorney) says " they have saved *Carlton, and have completely exonerated Mr. Knibb from having* EVER *said any thing to excite the rebellion.*"

On several estates in Trelawney, to the number of forty, or more, the members of my church mounted guard, and saved the property. Only three of the members were tried by Court Martial, *and they, I verily believe, were innocent.*

Not a single estate or pen was burnt where we had a member connected with Falmouth church, though the whole number was eighty-six.

On almost every estate that was saved from the rebels there were Baptists, and they were the cause of its being spared.

Several of the members have been rewarded by the House of Assembly for their good conduct.

Mr. Cantlow's church was in the heart of the rebellion; fifteen out of eighteen of his leaders were faithful to their owners. Of the other *three* we have no sufficient proof of guilt. A gentleman from America, who saw one of them tried and hung, said to me, I hope to meet him in heaven, he died for being a Baptist.

Many were actively engaged in saving property. Escrow Freeze, on Leyden Estate, has received his freedom for his good behaviour. His wife was shot, in her own house, by the troops. He was ordered to kill a negro, without trial, and refused, when the white man immediately chopped the negro to death.

William Ricketer, one of Mr. Burchell's deacons, saved the property from the rebels, when the troops ran away. I believe he has obtained his freedom.

After every exertion for the purpose, I could not find that *one* of Mr. Burchell's leaders or deacons was convicted of rebellion.

Not a single estate on which Mr. Abbott had members stopped work at all.

I could mention several other instances, but these will for the present suffice.

SECTION V.

Apprehended Illegality of the summary Proceedings against the Slaves during Martial Law.

The 80th Clause of the Consolidated Slave Law, passed 19th Feb. 1831, provides—

That if any slave or slaves shall, after the commencement of this act, enter into, or be concerned in, any rebellion or rebellious conspiracy, or commit any murder, felony, burglary, robbery, or set fire to any houses, out-houses, negro-houses, cane-pieces, grass or corn-pieces, or break into such houses, out-houses, or negro-houses, in the day time, no person being therein, and stealing thereout, or commit any other crime which would subject free persons to be indicted for felony, such slave or slaves shall, for every such offence or offences, upon trial and conviction thereof in manner hereinafter mentioned, suffer death, transportation, or such other punishment as the court shall think proper to direct, according to the nature and extent of the offence.

The 95th Clause enacts that—

Slaves are to be tried, &c. for crimes before courts of quarter sessions, or special slave courts, and by indictment before grand and petit juries. Sentence of death not to be carried into effect, but under governor's warrant, except in cases of rebellion.

Clause 108, provides—

That in all cases, where the punishment of death is inflicted, the execution shall be performed in a public part of the parish, and with due solemnity, or at such place in the parish as the Governor, or person executing the functions of governor, shall direct or appoint, and it shall be the duty of the rector or curate to prepare the criminal while under sentence, and to attend the place of execution; and care shall be taken by the gaoler or deputy-marshal that the criminal is free from intoxication at the time of his trial, and from thence to and at the time of his execution, under the penalty of twenty pounds; and the mode of such execution shall be hanging by the neck, and no other, and the body shall be afterwards disposed of as the court shall direct.

And Clause 136, enacts—

That the operation of this act, or any part thereof, shall not be suspended by Martial Law, any law, usage, or custom, to the contrary thereof in anywise notwithstanding.

It is a matter of notoriety that great numbers of negroes were executed by *sentence of Court Martial*, that many more were cruelly flogged, and that others were condemned to confinement in workhouses, and to be worked in chains for life, by the same tribunal.

Can we wonder that certain members of the House of Assembly were so eager to introduce a bill of indemnity for the militia?

It may be enquired, further, by whose authority the savage Maroons were commissioned to shoot whom they pleased, bringing in *the ears* of their victims as an evidence of their prowess?

We close this article by an extract of a letter relating to this subject from Mr. Whitehorne, dated 29th March, 1832.—

It may not be amiss to call your attention to the subject of the punishment of slaves during Martial Law. Perhaps you will see fit to direct the attention of the authorities to it. In the new Slave Law there are particular regulations for the trial by Jury of slaves for *rebellion, arson;* and there is also a clause to the effect, that the slave *law shall not be suspended during* Martial Law. Notwithstanding this, during the late business they were tried by *Military Courts,* shot, hanged, flogged, in the most summary manner. On the declaration of Martial Law, certain rules and articles of war came into operation—these are expressly for the government of the Militia, superseding during Martial Law the ordinary laws by which that body is regulated. Because, of the general word " whoever" in the 3rd and 4th Articles relating to rebellion, the Military thought proper to apply those clauses to *all classes,* though the preamble of the Act limits its contents to the Military only, and though the same expression "whoever" is used in other Articles (8. 15. 42. 6.) which relate to mere Military offences, and in others (2. and latter part of the 4th.) which apply to offences when committed by soldiers only, by the very terms used. The opinion of an intelligent legal friend coincides with mine, that none but the Military could be legally tried under these articles. Yet were the Missionaries laid hold of under them, and one (a Moravian) was actually tried— *and slaves were executed by hundreds.* Supposing, however, our opinions to be erroneous so far, they can scarcely be so on the following point. One of the Articles of War (38th) states, that " *No* corporal punishment shall be awarded under this act, or any other act, respecting the Militia, but imprisonment, or death." Yet, while professing to try people, both slaves and free, under this act, they did not hesitate to flog them to the extent of 300, many had 500 lashes, which is in breach of this clause. The general idea was, that all law was suspended, the Military took upon themselves the trial of whatever they considered offences, and punished them according to their arbitrary notions of their offensiveness. It made no difference that the Act charged was committed before Martial Law. A free man at Rio Bueno, (Mr. William Thompson) was taken up, his arms pinioned behind him. He was tried and threatened with the gibbet, for having been seen about a year before in the negro houses on an adjoining estate under circumstances that induced the suspicion that he had been *preaching!* Houses were pulled down in every direction, because (before Martial Law) they were used to *pray* in. Missionaries were threatened with imprisonment if they attempted to preach, and they were seized and treated as military offenders, on the charge that (before Martial Law) they had preached sedition. The hardship of trial by Court Martial is indescribable—the defence is so hindered that it is almost useless to make the attempt —the assistance of Counsel is denied, and altogether it is well described as an " apology for a trial." The friends of peace, order, and justice, ought to interfere to prevent a repetition of the gross outrages that have taken place, in case it should seem fit to Divine Wisdom to permit a recurrence of the late calamitous rebellion. It is a cry on every side that hundreds of innocent negroes were murdered, in the thirst for vengeance which pervaded the hearts of the whites. I think, for the protection of missionaries too, some stir should be made to prevent the abuses to which they have been subjected. The right to make us turn out, as soldiers, is very galling. Our horses, houses, and property were *selected* for the use of the soldiery, grossly injured, and remuneration in the ordinary way denied us, and our papers of the most delicate nature exposed to the inspection of every person who chose to order them to be seized.

At a SPECIAL MEETING *of the* DEPUTIES *from the several Congregations of* PROTESTANT DISSENTERS *of the three Denominations in, and within twelve miles of, London, appointed to protect their Civil Rights, held at the* KING'S HEAD TAVERN, *in the Poultry, on* THURSDAY, *the 26th day of* JULY, 1832, *for the purpose of taking into consideration various circumstances connected with the late insurrection in Jamaica, and the violations of Civil and Religious Liberty, which have been there perpetrated :*

HENRY WAYMOUTH, Esq. in the Chair.

RESOLVED,

THAT, as this Deputation was appointed for the express purpose of protecting the civil rights of Dissenters, it would be a dereliction of their duty not to declare their opinion on that open violation of these rights, which has lately taken place in Jamaica.

THAT it appears from accounts recently received from that island, that several Chapels, of the value of £23,000 currency, erected for the purpose of enabling the Negroes to attend religious worship, have been destroyed by an infuriated populace, led on and encouraged thereto, by some of the neighbouring magistrates and officers of militia. That, whilst one of the Missionaries has been imprisoned on bribed testimony, others have been treated with great brutality and cruelty, and that a system has been regularly organized to exclude from the island all Missionaries, whether of the Established Church, or of other religious societies.

THAT while this Meeting does not defend insurrection and incendiarism, on the part of the ignorant and degraded negroes, it cannot but severely reprobate the conduct of the magistrates and officers of militia, (who claim to be classed among the enlightened and civilized), as being unworthy any subject of the British empire—disgraceful to the age in which we live, and utterly subversive of the principles of Christianity.

THAT the principles of Christianity and slavery are so entirely opposed to each other, that the only remedy for these evils is the immediate and complete extinction of slavery; and that it is the opinion of this Meeting that in the approaching general election, it is the duty of every friend of humanity and of the Christian religion, to give a decided preference, in his vote, to those candidates who will support in Parliament, such measures as shall have for their end the accomplishment of this desirable object.

(Signed.)   HENRY WAYMOUTH, Chairman.

Teape and Son, Printers, Tower-hill.

A TREAD-MILL SCENE IN JAMAICA.

For an explanation of this Plate, see the Narrative of James Williams, advertised on the other side.

A

NARRATIVE OF EVENTS,

SINCE THE FIRST OF AUGUST, 1834,

By JAMES WILLIAMS,

AN APPRENTICED LABOURER IN JAMAICA.

LONDON:

PRINTED BY J. RIDER, 14, BARTHOLOMEW CLOSE.

PRICE SIXPENCE.

NARRATIVE, &c.

I am about eighteen years old. I was a slave belonging to Mr. Senior and his sister, and was brought up at the place where they live, called Penshurst, in Saint Ann's parish, in Jamaica.

I have been very ill treated by Mr. Senior and the magistrates since the new law come in. Apprentices get a great deal more punishment now than they did when they was slaves; the master take spite, and do all he can to hurt them before the free come;—I have heard my master say, "Those English devils say we to be free, but if we is to free, he will pretty well weaken we, before the six and the four years done; we shall be no use to ourselves afterwards."

Apprentices a great deal worse off for provision than beforetime; magistrate take away their day, and give to the property; massa give we no salt allowance, and no allowance at Christmas; since the new law begin, he only give them two mackarel,—that was one time when them going out to job.

When I was a slave, I never flogged,—I sometimes was switched, but not badly; but since the new law begin, I have been flogged seven times, and put in the house of correction four times.

Soon after 1st August, massa tried to get me and many

others punished; he brought us up before Dr. Palmer, but none of us been doing nothing wrong, and magistrate give we right.

After that, Mr. Senior sent me with letter to Captain Connor, to get punished, but magistrate send me back—he would not punish me, till he try me; when I carry letter back to massa, he surprise to see me come back, he been expect Captain Connor would put me in workhouse. Capt. Connor did not come to Penshurst; he left the parish. Massa didn't tell me what charge he have against me.

When Dr. Thompson come to the parish, him call one Thursday, and said he would come back next Thursday, and hold court Friday morning. He come Thursday afternoon, and get dinner, and sleep at Penshurst, and after breakfast, all we apprentices called up. Massa try eight of we, and Dr. Thompson flog every one; there was five man, and three boys: them flog the boys with switches, but the men flog with the Cat. One of the men was the old driver, Edward Lawrence; Massa say he did not make the people take in pimento crop clean; he is quite old—head quite white—havn't got one black hair in it, but Dr. Thompson ordered him to be flogged; not one of the people been doing any thing wrong; all flog for trifling, foolish thing, just to please the massa.

When them try me, massa said, that one Friday, I was going all round the house with big stone in my hand, looking for him and his sister, to knock them down. I was mending stone wall round the house by massa's order; I was only a half-grown boy that time. I told magistrate, I never do such thing, and offer to bring evidence about it; he refuse to hear me or my witness; would not let me speak; he sentence me to get 39 lashes; eight policemen was present, but magistrate make constable flog at first; them flog the old driver first, and me next; my back all cut up and cover with blood,—could not put on my shirt—but massa say, constable not flogging half hard enough, that my back not cut at all;—Then the magistrate make one of the police take the Cat to flog the other three men, and him flog most unmerciful. It was Henry James, Thomas Brown, and Adam Brown that the police flog.

Henry James was an old African; he had been put to watch large corn-piece—no fence round it—so the cattle got in and eat some of the corn—he couldn't help it, but magistrate flog him for it. After the flogging, he got quite sick, and begin coughing blood; he went to the hot-house,* but got no attention, them say him not sick.—He go to Capt. Dillon to complain about it; magistrate give him paper to carry to massa, to warn him to court on Thursday; that day them go to Brown's Town, Capt. Dillon and a new magistrate, Mr. Rawlinson, was there. Capt. Dillon say that him don't think that Henry James was sick; he told him to go back, and come next Thursday, and he would have doctor to examine him; the old man said he did not know whether he should live till Thursday; He walk away, but before he get out of the town, he drop down dead—all the place cover with blood that he puke up. He was quite well before the flogging, and always said it was the flogging bring on the sickness.

Same day Henry James dead, massa carry me and Adam Brown before magistrate; he said I did not turn out sheep till nine o'clock on Wednesday morning; I told magistrate the sheep was kept in to be dressed, and I was eating my breakfast before dressing them; but Capt. Dillon sentence me and Adam Brown to lock up in the dungeon at Knapdale for ten days and nights; place was cold and damp, and quite dark —a little bit of a cell, hardly big enough for me to lie full-length; them give we pint of water and two little coco or plantain a day;—hardly able to stand up when we come out, we was so weak; massa and misses said we no punish half enough; massa order we straight to our work, and refuse to let we go get something to eat.

The week after we let out of dungeon, Mr. Rawlinson come to Penshurst, and tell some of the people he not done with we yet about the sheep; we only put in dungeon for warning, and he would come back next Thursday, and try we again for it; He did come Thursday about four o'clock, and send call us, when we come, him and massa and misses was

* Hospital.

at dinner—we sent in to say we come—them said, Never mind till morning. We know this magistrate come to punish we for nothing, so we go over to Capt. Dillon at Southampton, to complain ; he write paper next morning to police-station, and policeman took us home. Mr. Rawlinson gone already; and Misses said he left order that we to lock up every night, and keep at work in day-time, till he come back—but police say no, Capt. Dillon order that we not to punish till he try we himself on Thursday, at Brown's Town ;—Them took us there, but Capt. Dillon did not come, but send paper for the other magistrate to try it, and said them couldn't try us for the same thing again. Mr. Rawlinson said it was not the same thing ; Mr. Senior said, No, we had been insolent to him ; we call constable to give evidence, and he said we not insolent ; Then magistrate say to Mr. Senior, " You mean insolence by manner." Massa answer, " Yes, that is what I mean, insolence by manner "—it was magistrate self that put massa up to say this ;—Then the magistrate sentence us to get twenty lashes apiece, which was given in front of court-house by police ; the punishment was very severe—both of us fainted after it—we lie down on the ground for an hour after it, not able to move ; A free man in the place sent some rum and camphor to bring we round. We went home that night, and went into hospital—them would hardly receive us, we stop there that night and Friday, lock up all day and night, and no feeding ; Saturday morning massa turned both of us out—we back all sore, quite raw, and we not able to stoop.

Ten days after the flogging at Brown's Town, Mr. Rawlinson come again to Penshurst on the Monday, and slept there. Next morning massa brought me up, and said that after the last punishment, when we get home, I did not turn out the horses and cows that night. I told magistrate I was sick with the flogging, and went to the hot-house, but Mr. Rawlinson order me twenty-five lashes for it ; Mr. Senior said, Let it be done on the place ;—Magistrate said yes, and ordered constable, William Dalling, to do it. I begg'd magistrate not to flog me again, as the other·flogging not well yet, but no use, he wouldn't hear me, but rode away from the place. Massa said he have no Cat, but he would find some switches to do it with; I was flogged with lancewood switches upon the old flogging—it tear off all the old scabs, and I not able to lie down on my back for two or three week after—was made to work with my back all sore.

About a month after the last flogging, massa said to me one day, that he would send for magistrate, and oblige him to do his duty, that all the gates in the pasture was down, and I never told him, and that I took up too much time to get in two turn of food for the horses; I said I couldn't do more than I was doing, I had too many things to do—first thing in the morning I had to blow shell, then to go to pasture and get in milking cow, and to milk them—then had to look over the sheep and cows, and all the stock, and to dress them that have sores—then to get them altogether, and give to one little boy to take them to pasture; at nine o'clock go to breakfast for half an hour, then have to go mend gaps in the stone wall, after that have to take two asses and a bill, to cut bread-nut food for the horses—had to climb the high trees to cut the bread-nut—then to chop it up, and load the two asses and take it home, and to come back for another load:—This finish between four and five, and by that time the little boy bring in all the cattle. I have to look over them and to turn them into different pastures, then have to go and get a bundle of wood for the watch-fire, and after that to supper the horses in the stable at night; they don't allow me to go to negro-houses—obliged to keep watch all night, sleeping in the kitchen, and to answer all call; Massa said I was only four years apprentice, and don't entitle to any time—that only one day in a fortnight due to me to work my ground and feed myself.

Massa never give me food; he allow me every other Sunday to work my ground, and sometimes he let me change it for another day. Magistrate say that was all the time the law allow.

As to the gates being down, massa go through them every day himself and see it; but he say I ought to have told him, and he will make magistrate punish me for it; him swear vengeance against me.

Mr. Rawlinson come on a Friday evening, and I was to have take next day for my day; but massa send me word that me not to take the day, as he want to bring me before the magistrate; I was frightened and didn't go next morning: Then I heard that magistrate said as I take the day against orders, when him and me meet he would· settle it: I was quite frightened when I hear this, and I go away to Spanish Town to see the governor—but didn't see him, as he was up in the mountain: I go back to Saint Ann's, and hide in the woods about Penshurst and Knapdale; I stop about seven weeks, and then go back to Spanish Town; I went to Mr. Ramsay, and he gave me paper to Mr. Emery, the Captain of Police, at St. Ann's—I met him on the road—he took me and put me in dungeon at Carlton—was kept there from Wednesday till Friday morning, then policeman came and took me to Brown's Town, and put me in cage till next day; then Mr. Rawlinson had me handcuffed and sent me to Penshurst, and put me in dungeon for ten days before he try me.

On the eleventh day Mr. Rawlinson came and slept there that night; next morning he had me brought out, and asked me about the running away, and I told him I go away because I was frightened when I hear how him and massa threaten me; then he sentenced me to St. Ann's Bay workhouse, for nine days, to get fifteen lashes in going in—to dance the treadmill morning and evening, and work in the penal gang; and after I come back from the punishment, I must lock up every night in dungeon till he visit the property again, and I have to pay fifty days out of my own time for the time I been runaway.

Then they handcuff me to a woman belonging to Little-field, to send to the workhouse; she have little child carrying on her back, and basket on her head, and when she want to give pickaniny suck, she obliged to rest it on one hand to keep it to the breast, and keep walking on; police don't stop to make her suckle the child. When we get to the workhouse, that same evening they give me the fifteen lashes; the flogging was quite severe and cut my back badly ; Then they put collar and chain upon my neck, and chain me to another man. Next morning they put me on the tread-mill along with the others : At first, not knowing how to dance it, I cut all my shin with the steps ; they did not flog me then—the driver shewed me how to step, and I catch the step by next day ; But them flog all the rest that could not step the mill, flogged them most dreadful. There was one old woman with grey head, belong to Mr. Wallace, of Farm, and she could not dance the mill at all : she hang by the two wrists which was strapped to the bar, and the driver kept on flogging her ;— she get more than all the rest, her clothes cut off with the Cat—the shoulder strap cut with it, and her shift hang down over that side—then they flog upon that shoulder and cut it up very bad ; but all the flogging couldn't make she dance the mill, and when she come down all her back covered with blood. They keep on putting her on the mill for a week, and flog her every time, but when they see she could not dance it, they stop putting her on ; if they no been stop, they would have kill her.

There was about thirty people in the workhouse that time, mostly men ; nearly all have to dance the tread-mill morning and evening ; six or eight on the tread-mill one time, and when them done, another spell go on, till them all done ; every one strap to the bar over head, by the two wrists, quite tight ; and if the people not able to catch the step, them hang by the two wrist, and the mill-steps keep on batter their legs and knees, and the driver with the cat keep on flog them all the time till them catch the step. The women was obliged to tie up their clothes, to keep them from tread upon them, while they dance the mill ; them have to tie them up so as only to reach down to the knee, and half expose themself ; and the man have to roll up their trowsers above the knee, then the driver can flog their legs with the cat, if them don't dance good ; and when they flog the legs till they all cut up, them turn to the back and flog away ; but if the person not able to dance yet, them stop the mill, and make him drop his shirt from one shoulder, so as to get at his bare back with the Cat. The boatswain flog the people as hard as he can lay it on—man and woman all alike.

One day while I was in, two young woman was sent in from Moneague side, to dance the mill, and put in dungeon, but not to work in penal gang; them don't know how to dance the mill, and driver flog them very bad ; they didn't tie up their clothes high enough, so their foot catch upon the clothes when them tread the mill and tear them ;—And then between the Cat and the Mill—them flog them so severe,—they cut away most of their clothes, and left them in a manner naked ; and the driver was bragging afterwards that he see all their nakedness.

Dancing tread-mill is very hard work, it knock the people up—the sweat run all down from them—the steps all wash up with the sweat that drop from the people, just the same as if you throw water on the steps.

One boatswain have to regulate the pole * of the mill, and make it go fast or slow, as him like; sometimes them make it go very fast, and then the people can't catch the step at all—then the other boatswain flogging away and cutting the people's legs and backs without mercy. The people bawl and cry so dreadful, you could hear them a mile off; the same going on every time the mill is about; driver keep the Cat always going while the people can't step.

When them come off the mill, you see all their foot cut up behind with the Cat, and all the skin bruise off the shin with the mill-steps, and them have to go down to the sea-side to wash away the blood.

After all done dance the mill, them put chain and collar on again, and chain two, three, and sometime four together, and turn we out to work penal gang—send us to different estate to work—to dig cane-hole, make fence, clean pasture, and dig up heavy roots, and sometimes to drag cart to bring big stone from mountain-side, about two or three miles from the bay; have to drag cart up steep hill. About ten o'clock they give we breakfast,—one quart of corn boiled up with a little

* The lever.

salt; sometime they give we a shad between two or three of we.

They keep us at work till between four and five o'clock, then take us back to the workhouse—take the chains off we all, and make us go upon the mill again, same fashion as in the morning. After that them put us into the bar-room—put the chain and collar on again, and our foot in the shackle-bar, to sleep so till morning. All the woman put into one room, and all the man in another; them that have any of the breakfast left from morning, them eat it after lock up, but them that eat all the allowance at breakfast, must starve till morning.

We keep on so every day till Sunday. Sunday the women sent to Mr. Drake's yard,* to clean it—and half the man go cut grass for his horses, and the other half carry water for the workhouse. After that they have to grind all the hoes, and the bills, and the axes, ready for Monday. Them work we all with the chains on, on Sunday, but they don't put us on tread-mill that day.

When the nine days done, them send me home; I so weak I hardly able to reach home; when I get there, Mr. Senior put me in the dungeon, and keep me there for four days and nights; he give me four little bananas and a piece of pumpkin with a little dry salt, and a pint of water. Magistrate didn't order me to be locked up in the day, only at night, but massa do it of his own will.

Then I begg'd massa to let me out, and I would do whatever I can to please him, and he do so, and order me to get bundle of wood and keep watch every night, instead of going to the dungeon.

After coming out of workhouse I never feel well, and about three weeks after, I got quite sick with fever and head-ache, and pain in the stomach; almost dead with the sickness. Massa told me one day, another punishment like that, and it will just do for me—it would kill me quite. Dr. Tucker pay good attention to me, and at last I get over it.

After this, it was long time before they punish me again,

---

* Mr. Drake is supervisor of the house of correction at St. Ann's Bay.

but they make me pay off the fifty days; them give me no Sunday at all; every Wednesday they give me half a day to work my grounds, the other half them take to pay off the fifty days;—For one year and three months, them keep on take the half day from me every week, and never give me any feeding.

In November, about five or six weeks before this last Christmas, one Friday, massa blow shell at nine o'clock for the gang to go to breakfast; it was the time them begin to get half Friday;—Them say no, they would rather work the four hours and a half one time, and then get the rest of the day. Joseph Lawrence, the constable, go to massa, and said the people would not go to breakfast, they wanted to work out the time at once. Massa said no, he would make them go to breakfast, and then work them till one o'clock. He ordered Lawrence to go away from the gang, and sent head constable, William Dalling, to order the people to breakfast; they said no, they would not; then massa go and order them himself, but they refused to go—then there was a great row and noise, and massa make them take up Joseph Lawrence the constable, and Thomas Brown; he say it must be them advise the people not to go to breakfast, and he put them in the dungeon—and he take William Mills and put in, because he don't go to breakfast, and Miss Senior call out for them to put in Benjamin Higgins, the old mason, for the same thing.

While massa was putting the people in the dungeon, I was passing from the pantry to the kitchen; Miss Senior was cursing at me, but I did not give any hearing to what she saying. Massa was standing near the kitchen—he ask me what I got to say about it; I say, Sir, I have nothing to do with it, I don't interfere; he say, You do interfere; I tell him no—he raise up his stick three times to lick me down. I said, you can't lick me down, sir, the law does not allow that, and I will go complain to magistrate if you strike me. He answer, he don't care for magistrate, he will lick the five pounds out of me that the magistrate will fine him:—Then he order me to be lock up along with the rest.

While they was putting me in, I said, "*It wasn't a man made this world, and man can't command it: the one that make the world will come again to receive it, and that is Jesus Christ!'* Massa called to William Dalling the constable, to bear witness what I was saying; he said he heard it, then they lock me up, and keep us there for twenty-four hours.

That same time massa sent for Mr. Rawlinson, he come Monday morning: four of us was tried, but he let off one and punish the other three. Massa tell the magistrate about the words I use—him tell the very words; magistrate ask me if I use them words? I tell him yes, but I wasn't mean any thing harm. Then him put constable on his oath, and he repeat the words I said; then Mr. Rawlinson told me I had no business to say so, and he sentence me to get twenty lashes in the workhouse, and to dance the treadmill morning and evening, and work in penal gang for seven days.

At same time him try Joseph Lawrence and his sister Amelia Lawrence. Massa said that on the Friday morning when he ordered Joseph Lawrence to go away from the gang, he disobeyed his order, and stopped at the gate. Mr. Rawlinson sentence him to get twenty lashes, and seven days in the workhouse, treadmill, and penal gang same as me, and he broke him from being constable, though he only swear him in for constable the Wednesday before.

When Amelia Lawrence was tried, massa said that every time he go to the field, he always find she at the first row, and he want to know what let she always take the first row—being her brother was the driver, she seem as if she want to take the lead. Amelia said massa ought to glad to see apprentice working at the first row, and doing good work. This was all the word that massa have to say against Amelia Lawrence, and Mr. Rawlinson sentence her to seven days in the workhouse, penal gang, and treadmill.

Amelia have four pickninys, two free and two apprentice, she left them with her family to take care of while she in the workhouse. Them put us all three together into dungeon after the court done, and send for police to carry we to workhouse. We kept in dungeon till next morning. Them don't give we a morsel to eat, and not a so so drop of water; but one of our friends, unknowing to massa, put a little victuals through a small hole.

In the morning three police take us out, and carry us down to the workhouse; them handcuff me and Joseph Lawrence together, and when we get there them take the handcuff off, and tie we up one after the other, and give we twenty lashes apiece : both of we very much cut up with the flogging. When the penal gang come back in the evening, them put us all on treadmill—after my back cut up that fashion, all over blood, it hurt me dreadful to dance the mill.

The workhouse was quite full this time, they hardly have enough collar and chain to put on all the people, they obliged to take off the collar and chain from some of the life people,* to put on the apprentice; and at night there wasn't enough shackle to fasten all the people, and hardly room enough for us all to lie down. There was a great many woman in the workhouse, and several have sucking child; and there was one woman quite big with child, and them make her dance the mill too morning and evening : she not able to dance good, and them flog her; she complain about her stomach hurt her, and I see her several time go and beg the overseer not to work her on the mill, but him say, not him send her there, and he must do his duty.

All the woman that not able to dance was flog most dreadful, in particular all the woman from Hiattsfield. There was twenty-one woman from Hiattsfield, and one man—several of them have young children; I think they was in for fourteen days. I found them in when I go there, and they was let out on Saturday night; I was present when they let out, and I hear the list call, and counted the people, and it was twenty-one woman from Hiattsfield.

When I go to the workhouse on the Tuesday, there was only three of these woman able to work in the field, all the rest was in the hospital, from being cut up with the mill and the flogging; them all look quite shocking when them let out, some hardly able to walk to go home, the most lively

* *Convicts* for life.

among them was all mashed up with the mill, all the skin bruised off her shin; she had a young child too: she tell me that she was put in workhouse three weeks before, and now them send her back again.

There was more than a hundred people in the workhouse this time—I reckon the life people and all; there was about seventeen or eighteen of them, and when penal gang turn out, them send ten or twelve of the life people along with apprentice, and all have to work together. The life people better treated more than apprentice; them get better feeding, them have quart of flour every second day instead of corn, and always get shad or salt fish every day; they don't put life people on treadmill, and I never see them put a lick upon one of the life people.

Almost every apprentice that sent to workhouse by magistrate, have to dance treadmill, except the sick in the hospital. It was miserable to see when the mill going, the people bawling and crying most dreadful—so they can't dance, so the driver keep on flogging; them holla out, " massa me no able! my 'tomach, oh! me da dead, oh!"—but no use, the driver never stop—the bawling make it rather worse, them make the mill go faster—the more you holla the more the mill go, and the driver keep on flogging away at all them not able to keep up; them flog the people as if them was flogging Cow.

One day one of the woman from Hiattsfield fainted on the mill; they been flogging at her, and the mill bruise all her shins; when she faint she drop off the mill, and look as if she dead; all her fellow apprentice set up crying, and ask if she going to dead left them; she not able to speak—two men carry her out into the yard, and lay her out upon the ground, and throw water upon her to bring her to; but for a long time them think she dead already; she didn't come to till next morning.

There was one old woman, name Sally, from Mr. Cohen's, at Cool Shade, was in workhouse when I go there, and she stop in there long time; she was in shocking condition—they had been putting her on the mill, and she don't able to dance at all, and them been flog her most terrible, but still she not able to dance, and at last them obliged to leave off putting her on the mill; but them keep on make her go out to work in penal gang, and chain her to one of the strong woman; She was badly treated more than any body I ever see in the workhouse; every day them flog her, she hardly able to stand. Two of the drivers, James Thomas, and Robert Lyne, make constant practice to flog this old woman, and Mr. Drake sometimes beat her himself with supple jack.

One day we was working at Banks's negro-houses, cutting Penguin to plant at Springfield—old Sally was chained to a young girl name Mary Murray; it was heavy rain time; driver was pushing the people on to run fast—was flogging them on, the young girl was trying to get on, and was hauling and dragging the chain that was on him and Sally neck, as Sally don't able to keep up; at last, the old woman fall down, right in a place where a stream of water was running through the negro-house street, and she don't able to get up again, then the driver stand over her with the cat, and flog her, but she not able to get up with the chain on, so he take off the chain, and make the young girl tie it round her body, and go along with the rest; then he stand over the old woman, and flog her with the cat till he make her get up, and keep on flogging at her till she get to the cook's fireside; the old creature stand there trembling, all wet up—for two or three hours she not able to move away, she look quite stupid; all the other people in the workhouse quite pity this poor old woman, it would make any body heart grieve to see her. The under-driver tell the head-driver one day, that if him keep on beat her so, some of these days she will dead under it, and then he will get into trouble; every day I was in the workhouse, except to Sunday, I see them beat this old woman, and I left her still in.

All the drivers and the boatswains in the yard, is people that sentence to the workhouse for life, two of them was very bad, them don't care how much them punish the apprentice.

Them woman that have young sucking child, have to tie them on their back, and go to the field chain two together; when it rain ever so hard they have to keep on work with the children tied on their backs, but when the weather dry, them put down the child at the fire-side; when Mr. Drake there, he don't allow them to suckle the child at all, if it cry ever so much; him say the children free, and the law don't allow no time to take care of them; it is only the good will of the driver that ever let woman suckle the children.

The drivers constant try to get after the young women that put into the workhouse,—even them that married, no matter; Before day in the morning, when the driver open the door to take the people out of the shackles, he call for any one he want, to come to his room, and many of them worthless ones do it; Amelia Lawrence complain to her brother and me, that never one morning pass without the driver after her—she don't know what to do, she quite hurt and disheated about it—but she did not give way; I heard him myself one morning calling her to come.

One day, Mr. Hilton, who is clerk in the Court-House,* come to the workhouse soon in the morning, while the tread mill was going. I been on already, but another spell was on, and Mr. Hilton take off one of the weights from the pole, and make the mill go faster; after him gone, some of the people tell me that in the afternoon he often come half-drunk, while the mill is going, then him take off the weight, and take off the man from the pole, and let the mill go flying round : When the pole let loose so, no person can step the mill—them all throw off, and hang by them two wrist, then him take the Cat in his own hand, and flog all the people with all his strength.

Them say that sometimes he drive out with his wife, and come round by the workhouse, and if the mill going, he will leave his wife in the gig, and go in to punish the people, and all the call his wife can call to him to leave off, no use.

On the Wednesday next week, they let us out,—we been sent for seven days, but they don't reckon the Sunday for one day; we reach home Thursday—I was quite weak with the flogging and the tread-mill, and the hard work in the penal gang; had a terrible pain in my stomach—hardly able

* Deputy Clerk of the Peace, perhaps.

to walk up hill; all the people that been flogged always complain of pain in the stomach.

The day after I come out of the workhouse, massa order me to go get bread-nut food for the horses. I said I was not able to climb tree; I was sick, and my shoulders was quite sore, and I could hardly use it, and I tell massa that this make six time that they flog me. He answer, he will make it ten times too, and if I sick, I must die. Every day he keep on order me to go for the bread-nut, but I was not able, and massa threaten me sorely—him tell me, that if I don't make an end of him, he will make an end of me.

On the Thursday next week, he told me he would take me to magistrate next day, and he swear very vengeance against me. I get frightened, and on Friday morning I go away to complain to the governor. When I get to Byndloss late at night, the overseer, Mr. Allen, meet me, and take me up, and put me in confinement till next morning, then he put me in charge of two constables, who carry me to police station, and the captain, Mr. Mackaw, put handcuffs on me, and sent me to the special magistrate at Linstead, and he put me in the workhouse, till massa should send for me; them chain me to another man, and make me work with the penal gang.

On Thursday, William Dalling, the constable, came for me, and them deliver me up to him. We set out, and walk most of the night—get to Walton school, and slept there; in the morning we start again, and reach home about twelve o'clock at night. On Saturday morning, William Dalling take me down to massa, and he send me on to Brown's Town; when the magistrate come, he shook his head at me, and said, Are you here again? Then they hold court. Massa said he ordered me to cut bread-nut, and I would not do it: me disobeyed his order, and on the Friday went away, and he did not see me again till this morning. I told magistrate that I did not cut bread-nut, because I was quite sick with my stomach, and massa threaten my life so hard, that make me go away to complain to the governor. Then the magistrate called the sergeant of police, and tell him, Lay hold of that fellow, and give him five-and-twenty good lashes—and after the flogging, I must be sent to workhouse again for *seven* days, and after I come out of the workhouse, I might go to the governor or whoever I like to complain. I told him the old flogging is not well yet, but he would not listen to me; They take me into the market-place, and tie me up to a tree, and give me the twenty-five lashes; all the people surprise to see them flogging me again, when the old one not well. The flogging was very severe; after it was done, I lay down before the door of the court-house, rain came on, and the police came and told me to go inside. I went in to where the court was sitting, and I said to Mr. Rawlinson, You don't do justice betwixt I and master. He tell me, that constable swear that I run away without a cause. I ask the constable, and he declare he never say any further than he took me out of Rodney Hall workhouse. Then Mr. Rawlinson say, I have been before him eight or nine times already; I say, If I have been twenty times before you, you ought to do justice 'twixt I and massa. He said, He do justice. I told him, You don't do justice. Then he said, If you say another word, I will put you out in the rain; then he made police take and handcuff me, to carry to workhouse. While I was standing outside the door, I hear massa say to Mr. Rawlinson, he had better let me stop in the workhouse for fourteen days; magistrate answer, That will make it till after new-year's-day; and then he said, Yes.

The policeman carry me to St. Ann's Bay, but night catch me in the pass, and police take me into Cardiff Hall, and we sleep there that night; next morning, Sunday, he take me on to workhouse, and I had to dance tread-mill and work penal gang like before.

The workhouse was nearly full like the last time, but most of them was different people—some that I left in I find still there; there was plenty of woman there, but only one have young child, that was Elizabeth Mason, from Mount Campbell, she was in for seven days to dance the tread-mill; she not able to dance good; after she been on little time, she miss step and drop, and hang by her two wrists, then the boatswain flog her with the Cat, as hard as he could put it,—then

c

she try to fetch up and catch the step, but fall again, and them keep on flog, and when they tire of flogging then they let her alone, and let the mill go on mashing her legs; all the skin was bruise off her shins, and her legs cut up with the Cat.

There was one young mulatto girl in for about ten days; she was name Margaret, and belong to Mr. Chrystie, the saddler, on the Bay; she complain of her stomach, and not able to dance the mill well; they flog her severe, and all her leg bruise with the mill; one evening her master come to the workhouse, when she was on the mill—he beg the boatswain to let the mill go fast, and flog Margaret well, and make her feel it, so that she will keep away from it after.

There was another woman from Drax Hall on the mill—she didn't dance good, and they flog her very much, and when she find the flogging come too hard, she call out, " Massa, me no one flesh, me two flesh;" she was in family way, but the overseer said he didn't care, it wasn't him give her belly, and after that they was harder upon her.

On Christmas day them make me and five other men go cut grass for Mr. Drake's horses, and some of the woman go clean his yard and carry water.

As magistrate been sentence me only for seven day, I ask the overseer on the Sunday if my time no up? He look at the book and say it was put down for fourteen day, so them keep me in till Tuesday night after New Year's day, that make two weeks and a half, for they don't count the Sunday.

There was one girl, named Mary Murray, in the workhouse same time as me, from Seville; she tell me not the magistrate write the paper for she to come to the workhouse—the busha write it, and shew it to magistrate, and him say it was all right; she tell we all, that what make them send her to workhouse was, that busha say the gang didn't turn out soon in the morning, and when the magistrate, Major Light, come, he send for the gang from the field, but them all frighten and run and hide—only she Mary Murray didn't run, and them take she before the magistrate, and send her straight off to the workhouse. All the people that speak to me, complain very bad about Major Light; them say him always drunk;—I see him drunk myself many times, going about the properties,—sometimes I see his servant obliged to hold him in the chaise, he was so drunk; him name is quite common for drunkard through the parish; them tell me that where him sleep, him put the room in such condition that they were obliged to clean it all out next morning.

When he go upon the estate he call to the overseer, Have you got any thing for me to do,—any person to flog? and if they tell him yes, then him stop, and if they give him rum to drink, he will do whatever thing them want him.

One day when I was working in penal gang, I saw six or seven of the Windsor apprentices, was going to the workhouse to be flogged—it was Major Light send them.

Another day I meet Major Light and the New Ground book-keeper coming down to the bay, and six men, hand-cuffed, and tied with rope, was following after, with two constable in charge of them; they was carried down to workhouse and flogged, and then sent back. Every body say them never see crueller man than Major Light—him in a manner begging the overseer to let him punish the people. Mr. Sowley was a king to Major Light.

The tread-mill at St. Ann's Bay, mash the people up quite dreadful; I see two woman at Knapdale, one named Nancy, married to Jarvis Webb, the other name Bessy, married to Philip Osborne; them been sent to dance tread-mill, and when them come back, all their legs bruise up, and make bad sore. I see them with bandage round their legs, and obliged to walk with stick; but the overseer and master no care for the work, or the time them lose, if them can only get the people well punish. Massa tell me to my face that he could do without me very well, if he could get me in the workhouse for six months.

One day Miss Senior say to me and some other apprentices, that Mr. Clarke, the busha at Knapdale, tell her that him send two woman to the tread-mill, and them come back so well hackled, that them not able to do nothing for three or four months, and she don't know what the devil in we, that we not well mashed up, when we come back from the tread-mill.

Mary Ann Bell, a mulatto girl, one of Miss Senior's house-servants, was quite large in the family way; Mr. Rawlinson sent her to dance the tread-mill, and when she come back she quite sick, and them strap her hand so tight upon the mill that she partly lost the use of her right hand ever since; she can't hold nothing heavy in that hand.

One day when I was at home in the pastures, close the public road, I see policeman carrying down an old man and a woman handcuffed together; the man was very old, he look more than sixty years old—he was all trembling, and hardly able to walk. I beg the police to stop and let me give them some orange; he do so, and the woman tell me that them sending her to the workhouse about her not delivering her free child to the overseer to let it work. I hear that many people begin to talk that the free child no have no right to stop on the property, and they will turn them off if the mothers don't consent to let them work; this woman come from Orange Valley, but I don't know anything more about her story.

The old man tell me that Mr. Rawlinson send him down to gaol, but him don't say what for; but about two months after I see him coming back from St. Ann's Bay. It was between Penshurst and Hinton Hill: him hardly able to crawl, his legs and back hackle most dreadful, and all his shirt and trowsers soak up with blood; I look at his right shoulder, and it was all in one sore, in a manner rotten up, with the flogging; I don't think him could live to reach home; he tell me he was two weeks coming from St. Ann's Bay (16 miles), obliged to beg victuals and shelter any place he come to. It was Mr. Rawlinson send him to gaol, and after he been there for a little time, them take him out and carry him before Mr. Sowley, and him put the old man in the workhouse.

Some of them magistrate don't care what them do to apprentice, as long as them can get good eating and drinking with the massa and busha, and sometimes them set the massa on to do worse than them want. All the apprentice say that

Major Light make it constant rule to do so, and myself see Mr. Rawlinson do so one time—it was the very morning them flog me with the lancewood switches; after the court over, Mr. Rawlinson order his mule ready to go away, and him and massa and Miss Senior was standing at the door; Misses was wanting something, and she call Nanny Dalling, when Nanny come, her face "tie up" *(i. e. looked sour or displeased)*—I believe she been have some dispute with her fellow servant outside ; Mr. Rawlinson say she look sulky and insolent, and him lay hold of her with him own hand, and haul her along to the dungeon, and push her in and lock the door; he left her child, a sucking baby, outside.

I was standing by the gate and see it all, and when Mr. Rawlinson mount his mule to go to Hinton Hill, I hear him say to massa, You must try to get up some good charge against that woman, and let me send her to the workhouse for about a fortnight; but massa answer that she have young child. The magistrate answer, That's no consequence; but massa didn't like to send her there. Mr. Rawlinson call again at Penshurst same day, as he coming back from Hinton Hill, and he make them bring Nanny Dalling out of the dungeon, and then he sentence her to be locked up in the duugeon for fourteen nights ; and them did lock her up every night along with her young pickniny.

As I tell about other things, I want to tell about one time I do something bad ; it was when massa get up a barrel of pork last year, in April; John Lawrence tell me he know where the pork was put, and he would help them with a part of it: two or three nights after they open the barrel, John Lawrence get a long stick, and tie a fork at the end of it, and then he go to the store window and stick the fork into the pork barrel, and get a piece of the meat and draw it to the window, but it couldn't come through the bars, so he come to the kitchen where I was sleeping, and he call me to come and help him; I go with him, and I hold the piece of pork while him cut it in two, and take and boil one half and give me some, and I eat it.

Misses and massa found out that the pork gone, and make

noise about it, and accuse all the house servant about it; I can't bear to hear them accuse for wrongful, and I know who did it, so I tell William Dalling the constable that I know all about the pork. Then him tell massa, and they call me up and I tell the truth, that John Lawrence tief the pork and I help him to cut it, and I eat some of it : them carry we before magistrate about it, and I tell Mr. Rawlinson the same thing, and John Lawrence confess it, and magistrate sentence John Lawrence and me to pay ten shillings a piece to massa for the pork: I borrow the money from my father and another man, and pay it to misses. This one bad action I do, them don't punish me for it.

It was the Tuesday evening after new year's day that they let me out of the workhouse, and I reach home next day. Miss Senior say them been looking out for me since last week, as I only sentence for seven days, and she think say, that I run away and go back to Rodney Hall again. She make pretence she don't know that magistrate alter it to four-teen days, and massa pretend the same, for him send William Dalling the constable to the magistrate the week before to say I don't come home yet, and him suppose me run away, but massa know very well that I was in the workhouse all the time.

Mr. Rawlinson self pretend him don't know I was in the workhouse so long, him say so to make William Dalling fool, because him was present when Mr. Rawlinson try me, and hear him sentence me to no more than seven days in the workhouse. Them don't know that I hear them make the bargain to keep me in all Christmas week.

Next time Mr. Rawlinson come to Penshurst massa try to get me punish again. Him say me didn't come home same day them let me out of the workhouse—he would have it me no come home till Thursday, but it was Wednesday, and I offer to call constable to prove it, and, at last, magistrate put an ending to it, and told massa he must accuse me wrongfully.

This was the last time they carry me before Mr. Rawlinson, and that was last January.

One Saturday afternoon, about the end of February, Philip Osborn of Knapdale came to me, and say that James Finlayson want to see me at Brown's Town that night. James Finlayson was my fellow apprentice before time, but been buy himself free, and he was a leader in the church. He send tell me that two gentlemen was there that want to ask how apprentice treated, and him know me been treated very badly, so him send for me.

At night I go to the chapel, and see Mr. Sturge and Mr. Harvey, and I tell them all about my bad living; Mr. Sturge tell me, me mustn't discourage, that it only to last seventeen months; I tell him, I don't know if I can live to see the seventeen months out; I was quite maugre and hungry that time, quite different to what I stand now, I hardly able to get anything to eat then, my ground all gone to pieces, the time them put in workhouse, and if my father and other people no been give me something, I would have starve. Mr. Sturge give me a shilling, and then I go back home.

On Monday night, Finlayson send for me again, I go Tuesday night, and he send me to Mr. Clarke, the minister. Him ask me if me would like to be free, I tell him, Yes, and him ask me if I would pay him back when me free? I said, Yes, I would do all in my power, and try my best endeavour to work hard and pay him back. Then Mr. Clarke tell me I must go to magistrate, to give warning to have me valued; I was quite happy and joyful, when I hear this; and on Saturday, I go to Mr. Rawlinson, at Brown's Town, and ask him to value me, but him say massa entitle to fourteen days' warning; he give me paper to serve massa, about it, and said he would very glad if I could buy myself, as he have more trouble with me and massa than any body else. I give the paper to misses, as massa was in Spanish Town, and second Saturday after, I go to Brown's Town, to be valued; but when I get there, Mr. Rawlinson tell me, as massa don't come, he couldn't value me, and all I can say no use, he keep on refuse to value me; then I go to Mr. Clarke, the minister, and he come to the Court House, and speak to Mr. Rawlinson, and at last he agree to go on with the valuation.

Him and Mr. Abraham Isaacs and Mr. Fairweather value

me; Mr. Joseph Isaacs, that keep a store at Brown's Town, give evidence. He say he want a boy like me, to mind his horse, and follow him to town, and when me free, he would be willing to give me two dollars a week, and feeding and clothes besides; so them fix the price upon me for eight doubloons, ten dollars and a half, and two bitts.*

After it done, Mr. Clarke take me to his house, and give me the money, and I carry it straight to Mr. Rawlinson, and then he give me my free paper, and when I come out of the Court House, I call out, quite loud, " Bless God Almighty—thank the Lord, I get out of devil's hands." Mr. Clarke, the Busha at Knapdale, was present—he look quite black at me, but him don't speak.

Then I go straight to Mr. Joseph Isaacs' store, and I tell him, I going to come to him Monday, as he say him would give me two dollars a week, and feeding and clothes; he tell me he get a boy already, but he don't get any—he only take swear he would give that, to make them put high value upon me.

Then Mr. Clarke, the minister, told me, it was Mr. Sturge that pay the money for me, and I must go to him at Spanish Town, as he want to carry me to England.

I feel so happy, I don't know what to do with myself hardly; I bless the Lord; and I bless Mr. Sturge for him goodness. If he no been take me away, I couldn't have live long.

On Tuesday I start off, and get to Spanish Town next day, after that we go to Kingston; and two weeks after, Mr. Sturge take me with him on board the ship, and we go to New York, and then sail to Liverpool, and so here I am in England.

---

* That is £46. 4s. 7d. Jamaica currency, for one year and five months' service !

The ordinary wages of a good *house* domestic in Jamaica, is a dollar and a half per week, out of which the servant is allowed half a dollar for his own support. A valuation according to this standard, together with the usual deduction of one-third for contingencies, would have brought the true value of James Williams's services to about the sum of £15. for the unexpired term of the apprenticeship !

The foregoing narrative has been carefully taken down from the lips of the narrator—his own peculiar style being faithfully adhered to.

Joseph Sturge has in his possession a document, signed by six members of a Christian church, who had all known James Williams for several years, and in that document they bear testimony to his character for veracity.

Horrible and afflicting as is this picture of negro-suffering, since the pretended Abolition of Slavery; it bears the strong impress of self-evident truth and fidelity ; additional and corroborative evidence, however, will not be wanting in proper season, shewing that this is but a sample of the general system—that cruelties and atrocities in various forms and modifications are now being perpetrated throughout several of our larger colonies.

Let it not be forgotten, that the people of England have paid twenty millions for the abolition of slavery, and that a large amount is still being annually drawn from the public revenue, for the support of more than one hundred stipendiary magistrates !

Yet, notwithstanding this costly—this monstrous sacrifice of British treasure, the object for which that sacrifice was made, has never been attained—*slavery has not been abolished* —it exists with unmitigated rigour, in its most ferocious, revolting, and loathsome aspect.

Cruelties unheard of—unthought of in the worst days of slavery, are now being "heaped like burning coals" on the heads of the long suffering, and patiently enduring sons and daughters of Africa.

And will the people of England look tamely on, and accede to this as the fruition of their benevolent desires ? Will they calmly brook the glaring insult offered—the treacherous fraud practised, by the open and flagitious violation of a solemn compact? And will the people of England permit the deeply injured, the helpless, the unoffending negro, still to remain the victim of such accumulated misery and brutal outrage ?

No! It must not be—the voice of justice, humanity and religion sternly demands that effectual steps be taken to secure full and immediate retribution;—we ask not the disgorgement of the misapplied twenty millions, but we demand the fulfilment of the bond—the ransom has been paid, but the captive is still retained in his galling fetters!

There is but one remedy—half measures are worse than useless— it requires but a single, brief, simultaneous and energetic movement, and the struggle is over. Immediately re-organize your Anti-Slavery Societies—let the country be aroused—and let the people, with one voice, instruct their representatives peremptorily to demand the instant, the unconditional, and the everlasting annihilation of the accursed system.

June 1st, 1837.

J. Rider, Printer, 14, Bartholomew Close, London.